STARTING TO UNIT TEST:

Not as Hard as You Think

STARTING TO UNIT TEST:

Not as Hard as You Think

ERIK DIETRICH

CONTENTS

CHAPTER 1

DON'T WORRY, YOUR SECRET IS SAFE WITH ME

Have you ever been introduced to someone and promptly forgotten their name? Or have you ever worked with someone or seen someone enough socially that you ought to know his name but don't? He knows yours, and you're no longer in a position where it's socially acceptable for you to ask him his. You're stuck. Now you're sentenced to an indefinite period of either avoiding calling him by name, avoiding him altogether, or awkwardly trying to get someone else to say his name. Through little to no fault of your own, you're going to be punished socially for an indefinite period of time.

I think the feeling described strongly parallels the feeling that a developer has when the subject of unit testing comes up. Maybe it's broached in an interview by the interviewer or interviewee. Perhaps it comes up when a new team member arrives or when you arrive as the new team member. Maybe it's at a conference over drinks or at dinner. Someone asks what you do for unit testing, and you scramble to hide your dirty little secret – you don't have the faintest idea how it works. I say that it's a dirty little secret because, these days, it's generally industry-settled case law that unit testing is what the big boys do, so you need either to be doing it or have a reason that you're not. Unless you come up with <u>an awesome lie</u>.

The reasons for not doing it vary. "We're trying to get into it." "I used to do it, but it's been a while." "Oh, well, sometimes I do, but sometimes I don't. It's hard when you're in the [insert industry here] industry." "We have our own way of testing." "We're going to do that starting next month." It's kind of like when dentists ask if you're flossing. But here's the thing. Like flossing, (almost) nobody really debates the merits of the practice. They just make excuses for not doing it.

I'm not here to be your dentist and <u>scold you for not flossing</u>. Instead, I'm here to be your buddy: the buddy with you at the party that knows you don't know that guy's name and is going to help you figure it out. I'm going to provide you with a survival guide to getting started with unit testing – the bare essentials. It is my hope that you'll take this and get started following an excellent practice. But if you don't, this will at least help you fake it a lot better at interviews, conferences and other discussions.

Let's Get our Terminology Straight

One common pitfall for the unit-test-savvy faker is misuse of the term. Nothing is a faster giveaway that you're faking it than saying that you unit test and proceeding to describe something you do that isn't unit testing. This is akin to claiming to know the mystery person's name and then getting it wrong. Those present may correct you or they may simply let you embarrass yourself thoroughly.

Unit testing is testing of units in your code base – specifically, the most granular units or the building blocks of your application. In theory, if you write massive, procedural constructs, the minimum unit of code could be a module. But in reality, the unit in question is a class or method. You can argue semantics about the nature of a unit, but this is what people who know what they're talking about in the industry mean by unit test. It's a test for a class and most likely a specific method on that class.

Here are some examples of things that are not unit tests and some good ways to spot fakers very quickly:

1. Developer Testing. Compiling and running the application to see if it does what you want it to do is not unit testing. A lot of people, for some reason, refer to this as unit testing. You can now join the crowd of people laughing inwardly as they stridently get this wrong.

2. Smoke/Quality Testing. Running an automated test that chugs through a laundry list of procedures involving large sections of your code base is not a unit test. This is the way the QA department does testing. Let them do their job and you stick to yours.

3. Things that involve databases, files, web services, device drivers or other things that are external to your code. These are called integration tests and they test a lot more than just your code. The fact that something is automated does not make it a unit test.

So what is a unit test? What actually happens? It's so simple that you'll think I'm kidding. And then you'll think I'm an idiot. Really. It's a mental leap to see the value of such an activity. Here it is:

| 1 | ```
[TestMethod, Owner("ebd"),
TestCategory("Proven"),
``` |
| 2 | ```
TestCategory("Unit")]
``` |
| 3 | ```
public void Returns_False_For_1()
``` |
| 4 | ```
{
``` |
| 5 | ```
    var finder = new PrimeFinder();
``` |
| 6 | ```
    Assert.IsFalse(finder.IsPrime(1));
``` |
| | ```
}
``` |

I instantiate a class that finds primes, and then I check to make sure that IsPrime(1) returns false, since one is not a prime number. That's it. I don't connect to any databases or write any files. There are no debug logs or anything like that. I don't even iterate through all of the numbers one through 100, asserting the correct thing for each of them. Two lines of code and one simple check. I am testing the smallest unit of code that I can find – a method on the class yields X output for Y input. This is a unit test.

I told you that you might think it's obtuse. I'll get to why it's obtuse like a fox later. For now, let's just understand what it is. This way, at our dinner party we're at least not blurting out the wrong name, unprovoked.

What is the Purpose of Unit Testing?

Unit testing is testing, and the purpose of testing a system is to ensure quality. Right? Well, not so fast.

Testing is, at its core, experimentation. We're just so used to the hypothesis that our code will work and that tests will confirm that to be the case (or prove that it isn't, resulting in changes until it does) that we equate testing with its outcome – quality assurance. And we generally think of this occurring at the module or system level.
```

Testing at the unit level is about running experiments on classes and methods and capturing those experiments and their results via code. In this fashion, a sort of "state of the class" is constructed via the unit test suite for each unit-tested class. The test suite documents the behavior of the system at a very granular level and, in doing so, provides valuable feedback as to whether or not the class's behavior is changing when changes are made to the system.

So unit testing is part of quality assurance, but it isn't *itself* quality assurance, per se. Rather, it's a way of documenting and locking in the behavior of the finest-grained units of your code – classes – in isolation. By understanding exactly how all of the smallest units of your code behave, it is straightforward to assemble them predictably into larger and larger components and thus construct a well-designed system.

Some Basic Best Practices and Definitions

So now that you understand what unit testing is and why people do it, let's look at some basic definitions and generally accepted practices surrounding unit tests. These are the sort of things you'd be expected to know if you claimed unit testing experience.

- Unit tests are just methods that are decorated with annotations (Java) or attributes (C#) to indicate to the unit test runner that they are unit tests. Each method is generally a test.

- A unit test runner is simply a program that executes compiled test code and provides feedback on the results.

- Tests will generally either pass or fail, but they might also time out or be inconclusive, depending on the tooling that you use.

- Unit tests (usually) have "Assert" statements in them. These statements are the backbone of unit tests and are the mechanism by which results are rendered. For instance, if there is some method in your unit test library Assert. IsTrue(bool x) and you pass it a true variable, the test will pass. A false variable will cause the test to fail.

- The general anatomy of a unit test can be described using the mnemonic AAA, which stands for "Arrange, Act, Assert." What this means is that you start off the test by setting up the class instance in the state you want it (usually by instantiating it and then whatever else you want), executing your test and then verifying that what happened is what you expected to happen.

- There should be one assertion per test method the vast majority of the time, not multiple assertions. And there should (almost) always be an assertion.

- Unit tests that do not assert will be considered passing, but they are also spurious since they don't test anything. (There are exceptions to this, but that is an intermediate topic and in the early stages you'd be best served to pretend that there aren't.)

- Unit tests are simple and localized. They should not involve multi-threading, file I/O, database connections, web services, etc. If you're writing these things, you're not writing unit tests but rather integration tests.

- Unit tests are fast. Your entire unit test suite should execute in seconds or quicker.

- Unit tests run in isolation, and the order in which they're run should not matter at all. If test one has to run before test two, you're not writing unit tests.

- Unit tests should not involve setting or depending on global application state such as public, static, stateful methods, singletons, etc.

Lesson One Wrap Up

Hopefully, if you've been faking it all along with unit tests, you can now at least fake it a little bit better by actually knowing what they are, how they work, why people write them and how people use them. Perhaps together we can get you started adding some value by writing them, but at least for now this is a start.

CHAPTER 2

LET'S WRITE A TEST

In the previous chapter, I talked about what unit testing is and isn't, what its actual purpose is, and what some best practices are. This is like explaining the Grand Canyon to someone that isn't familiar with it. You now know enough to say that it's a big hole in the earth that provides some spectacular views and that you can hike down into it, seeing incredible shifts in flora and fauna as you go. You can probably convince someone you've been there in a casual conversation, even without having seen it. But you won't really get it until you're standing there, speechless. It's the same with unit testing. You won't really get it until you do it and get some benefit out of it.

So, Let's Write that Test

Let's say that we have a class called PrimeFinder. (Anyone who has watched my Pluralsight course will probably recognize that I'm recycling the example class from there.) This class's job is to determine whether or not numbers are prime, and it looks like this:

```
 1    public class PrimeFinder
      {
 2        public bool IsPrime(int possiblePrime)
 3        {
 4            return possiblePrime != 1 && !Enumerable.
 5    Range(2, (int)Math.Sqrt(possiblePrime) - 1).Any(i
 6    => possiblePrime % i == 0);
 7        }
      }
```

Wow, that's pretty dense looking code. If we take the method at face value, it should tell us whether a number is prime or not. Do we believe the method? Do we have any way of knowing that it works reliably, apart from running an entire application, finding the part that uses it and poking at it to see if anything blows up? Probably not, if this is your code and you needed my last chapter to understand what a unit test was. But this is a pretty simple method in a pretty simple class. Doesn't it seem like there ought to be a way to make sure it works?

I know what you're thinking. You have a scratchpad and you copy and paste code into it when you want to experiment and see how things work. Fine and good, but that's a throwaway effort that means nothing. It might even mislead when your production code starts changing. And checking might not be possible if you have a lot of dependencies that come along for the ride.

But never fear. We can write a unit test. Now, you aren't going to write a unit test just anywhere. In Visual Studio, what you want to do is create a unit test project and have it refer to your code. So if the PrimeFinder class is in a project called Daedtech.Production, you would create a new unit test project called DaedTech.Production. Test and add a project reference to Daedtech.Production. (In Java, the convention isn't quite as cut and dry, but I'm going to stick with .NET for this example). You want to keep your tests out of your production code so that you can deploy without also deploying a bunch of unit test code.

Once the test class is in place, you write something like this, keeping in mind the Arrange, Act, Assert paradigm described in the previous chapter:

1	[TestMethod]
2	public void Returns_False_For_One()
3	{
4	var primeFinder = new PrimeFinder(); //Arrange
5	
6	bool result = primeFinder.IsPrime(1); //Act
7	
8	Assert.IsFalse(result); //Assert
9	}

The TestMethod attribute is something that I described in the last chapter. This tells the test runner that the method should be executed as a unit test. The rest of the method is pretty straightforward. The arranging is just declaring an instance of the class under test (commonly abbreviated CUT). Sometimes this will be multiple statements if your CUTs are more complex and require state manipulation prior to what you're testing. The acting is where we test to see what the method returns when we pass it a value of one. The asserting is the Assert.IsFalse() line where we instruct the unit test runner that a value of false for result means the test should pass, but true means that it should fail since one is not prime.

Now, we can run this unit test and see what happens. If it passes, that means that it's working correctly, at least for the case of one. Maybe once we're convinced of that, we can write a series of unit tests for a smattering of other cases in order to convince ourselves that this code works. And here's the best part: when you're done exploring the code with your unit tests to see what it does and convince yourself that it works (or perhaps you find a bug during your testing and fix the code), you can check the unit tests into source control and run them whenever you want to make sure the class is still working.

Why would you do that? Well, might be that you or someone else later starts playing around with the implementation of IsPrime(). Maybe you want to make it faster. Maybe you realize it doesn't handle negative numbers properly and aim to correct it. Maybe you realize that method is written in a way that's clear as mud and you want to refactor toward readability. Whatever the case may be, you now have a safety net. No matter what happens, one will never be prime, so the unit test above will be good for as long as your production code is around – and longer. With this test, you've not only verified that your production code works now; you've also set the stage for making sure it works later.

Resist the Urge to Write Kitchen Sink Tests

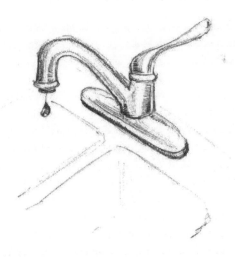

When I talked about a smattering of tests, I bet you had an idea. I bet your idea was this:

```
1    [TestMethod]
2    public void Test_A_Bunch_Of_Primes()
3    {
4        var primes = new List<int>() { 2, 3, 5, 7, 11,
5    13, 17 };
6        var primeFinder = new PrimeFinder();
7
8        foreach(var prime in primes)
9            Assert.IsTrue(primeFinder.IsPrime(prime));
10   }
```

After all, it's wasteful and inefficient to write a method for each case that you want to test when you could write a loop and iterate more succinctly. It'll run faster and it's more concise from a coding perspective. It has every advantage that you've learned about in your programming career. This must be good. Right?

Well, not so much, counterintuitive as that may seem. In the first place, when you're running a bunch of unit tests, you're generally going to see their result in a unit test runner grid that looks something like a spreadsheet. Or perhaps you'll see it in a report. If when you're looking at that, you see a failure next to "IsPrime_Returns_False_For_12" then you immediately know, at a glance, that something went wrong for the case of 12. If instead you see a failure for "Test_A_Bunch_Of_Primes", you have no idea what happened without further investigation. Another problem with the looping approach is that you're masking potential failures. In the method above, what information do you get if the method is wrong for both two and 17? Well, you just know that it failed for something. So you step through in the debugger, see that it failed for two, fix that and move on. But then you wind up right back there because there were actually two failures, though only one was being reported.

Unit test code is different from regular code in that you're valuing clarity and the capture of intent and requirements over brevity and compactness. As you get comfortable with unit tests, you'll start to give them titles that describe correct functionality of the system and you'll use them as kind of a checklist for getting code right. It's like your to-do list. If every box is checked, you feel pretty good. And you can put checkboxes next to statements like "Throws_Exception_When_Passed_A_Null_Value" but not next to "Test_Null".

There are some very common things that new unit testers tend to do for a while before things click. Naming test methods things like "Test_01⊠ and having dozens of asserts in them is very high on the list. This comes from heavily procedural thinking. You'll need to break out of that to realize the benefit of unit testing, which is inherently modular because it requires a complete breakdown into components to work. If nothing else, remember that it's, "Arrange, Act, Assert," not, "Arrange, Act, Assert, Act, Assert, Assert, Assert, Act, Act, Assert, Assert, Act, Assert, etc."

Wrap Up

The gist of this chapter is that unit tests can be used to explore a system, understand what the system does and then guard to make sure the system continues to work as expected even when you and others are in it making changes later. This helps prevent unexpected side effects during later modification (i.e., regressions). We've also covered that unit tests are generally small, simple and focused, following the Arrange, Act, Assert pattern. No one unit test is expected to cover much ground – that's why you build a large suite of them.

CHAPTER 3

UNIT TESTING SUCKS

I don't know about you, but I remember desperately wanting to be able to drive right up until I was fifteen years old and I got my learner's permit. I thought about it a lot – how fun it would be, how much freedom I would have, how my trusty old bike would probably get rusty from disuse. About a month after getting my permit, I desperately wanted my license and to drive on my own without supervision. But I'm omitting a month there, during which an unexpected thing happened. I realized that driving was stupid and awful and it sucked and I hated it and I'd never do it, so just forget it!

It was in that month that the abstraction of operating a car and having freedom became the reality of hitting the gas when I meant to hit the brake pulling out of my driveway or not knowing when I was supposed to go after stopping at a stop sign. It was a weird mix of frustration, anger and fear that tends to accompany new activities – even ones that you know will benefit you. I titled this chapter not intending to satirize a position but to empathize with a position. Like many things when you're new to them, starting to unit testing quite frankly sucks. It's frustrating, foreign and hard to get right. Accordingly, it's easy to abandon it when you have deadlines to meet.

This chapter is about minimizing frustration and barriers to adoption by staying focused and setting reasonable expectations. I would argue that if you're new to writing tests, writing a few and enjoying localized success without high coverage is a lot more important than suddenly becoming a test-driven development (TDD) expert with 100% test coverage right out of the gate (or at least trying to become one). Incremental progress is good.

Don't Try TDD Just Yet

I'm a little torn as I write this, but the first thing that I'll suggest is that you not try TDD if you have no experience unit testing. Some might disagree with this suggestion, but I think that you're going to be trying to learn too many new things all at once and will be a lot more likely to get frustrated. Unit tests are simply pieces of code that you write, as covered in more detail in the last chapter. It's a new kind of code to be writing, but you're just learning about new methods to call and attributes (or annotations, in Java) to use. You'll get there.

But TDD is an entirely new way of writing code. It's a discipline in which you do not write any production code until you have written a unit test that fails. Then you get that test and all other tests to pass and refactor the code as needed. Does that sound crazy (if you discount the fact that a number of developers you respect probably do it)? Exactly. Probably not for you right now. It's a bridge too far, and you're more likely to throw up your arms in disgust and quit if you try to learn both things right now. I speak from experience, as years ago I was introduced to unit testing and TDD at the same time. I was overwhelmed until I just went back to figuring out the whole unit testing thing alone first. Maybe that wouldn't happen to you, but I'd caution you to be wary of learning these two things simultaneously.

So let's stick to learning what unit tests are and how to write them.

Test New Classes Only

In my Pluralsight course, I use the example of a method that identifies numbers as prime or not, and in a series of blog posts I did last fall on TDD, I use the example of something that calculates a bowling score. I've also done other code katas and exercises like these in the past to show people both the mechanics of unit testing and TDD.

When I do this, one of the things people frequently say is something along the lines of "pff...sure, when you're writing something stupid and easy like a prime number finder, but there's no way that would work on our code base." I then surprise these people by agreeing with them. I'm sure it wouldn't work on your code base. Why? Well, because unit tests don't just magically spring up like mushrooms after a few days of rain. They're more like roses

– you have to plan for them from the start and carefully cultivate an environment in which they can thrive.

Some years back, I saw an <u>excellent talk</u> by Michael Feathers called "The Deep Synergy Between Testability and Good Design." I highly suggest watching this talk if you haven't seen it, but to summarize, he states (and I agree) that well-designed and factored code goes hand in hand with testability. You're much more likely to find that code written to be testable is good code, and, conversely, code written without unit tests in mind is not the greatest. And so if you're deeply invested in a code base that has never been covered by unit tests, it doesn't surprise me to hear that you don't think unit testing would work on your code. I imagine it wouldn't.

But don't throw out unit testing because it looks like it wouldn't work in your code base. Just resolve to do it on new classes that you create. As you go along and get better at unit testing, you'll start to understand how to write testable classes. It will thus get easier and easier to test all new additions to the code, and you'll start to get the hang of it with relatively minimal impact on your existing code, your process or your time. Starting to unit test doesn't mean that you're suddenly responsible for testing every line of code in history, nor does it mean you must test every single new line. Just start out by writing a few that you think will help.

Test Existing Code by Extracting Little Classes

Once you get the feel for adding unit tests for new classes/code that you add to the code base, it's a good time to start taking baby steps toward getting tests in place for your legacy (non-tested) code. Now, some procedural, monolithic mass of code that wasn't testable a month ago when you started out isn't magically testable now because you have some practice. It's still a problem.

You're going to have to chip away at it. And you're going to have to do this by developing a new skill: identifying pieces of functionality that you can pull out into new classes and test. Go look through methods and classes and find things that don't have a lot of dependencies on class fields or (yuck) global/static variables. Excellent candidates for this are methods with pure in-memory operations and ones that deal largely with primitives. Do you have some gigantic method that has a whole region buried in it that does nothing but cobble together a string to be used later in the method? Pull that out into a new class and write unit tests that make assertions about the string it returns.

As you practice this, you'll get a better and better feel for what you can pull out with a minimum of friction. You'll find yourself not only getting more of your code base under test but also improving its design and modularity.

Know When to Fold 'Em

This is another one that's hard to type, but you have to learn to look at code and say, "nope, not happening." There are classes and methods that you simply are not going to be able to test unless you come back with a green belt in unit testing – or pair with someone who has hers. And even then, the prognosis may be that you need to rewrite the legacy class/method altogether to make it testable. Here is a quick list of things that, early in your unit-testing career, you should consider to be deal-breakers and simply move on from to avoid frustration. As a beginner, avoid testing code (class methods and properties) that does the following:

1. Calls static methods. At best, a static method is <u>function-al</u> and returns something that depends only on its inputs. If this is the case (as it is with functions like Math.Pow() or Math.Abs()), the code is still testable. But a far more common case, especially if the static methods are ones in your own code base, is that they manipulate some kind of global state. Global state is testability kryptonite. I'll explain more later, but for now, please take my word for it.

2. Invokes <u>singletons</u>. The singleton design pattern is used almost universally as a politically correct way to hide your global variables in plain sight. For what this means to testability, see the last bullet. If it calls singletons, forget it, move on.

3. Dispatches background workers or manages threading. When unit tests are run, the unit test runner is responsible for managing threading and it will run your tests in parallel. If you're trying to make sure your threads and thread management are in one state for production and another for testing, you are about to ruin your day and probably your week. It's not worth it – don't try.

4. Accesses files, connects to databases, calls web services, etc. I mentioned this in the first chapter, but that was in the context of saying that these things aren't considered unit tests. Well, another issue here is that they're also relatively brittle and long running. If you write tests that do these things, they're going to fail at weird times and in unpredictable ways. You'll be used to all of your tests passing and suddenly one fails and then passes again, and it turns out it's because Bill from accounting bumped into the database server and its Nic card is a little "tricky." If you have unit tests that fail for borderline inconceivable reasons beyond

your control, you will become discouraged.

5. Triggers any of the above anywhere in the call stack. You don't escape the problems of threading, global state or externalities by not using them directly. If you trigger them, it's the same difference.

6. Has classes that require crazy amounts of instantiation. If you want to test a method but it has forty-five parameters, most of which are classes that are difficult or complex to create, forget it. That code sorely needs reworking, and creating massive, brittle tests for it this early in your unit-testing career will be a world of pain. Chip away at making the design better before you tackle it.

Don't worry – I'm not suggesting that you give up on a long timeline, and I'll discuss strategy for addressing these things later. But for now, just consider them signals that this code is out of bounds for testing. If you don't, there's a high likelihood that you'll spin your wheels and get angry, frustrated and irritable. This in turn makes it more likely that you'll give up. I can't eliminate the frustration of being new at something like driving, but I can at least steer you away from six-way traffic lights and three-lane roundabouts.

CHAPTER 4

DESIGN NEW CODE FOR TESTABILITY

In the last chapter, I covered what I think of as an important yet seldom-discussed subject: how not to overwhelm yourself and get discouraged when you're starting to unit test. In the chapter before that, I showed the basics of writing a unit test. But this leaves something of a gap. You can now write a unit test in a vacuum for an extremely simple class, and when looking at your legacy code base, you know what to avoid. But you don't necessarily how to write a non-trivial application with unit tests.

You might understand now how to write tests, assuming that you have some disconnected new class in your code base without dependencies and barriers to testing, but you wonder how to get to that point in the first place. I mean, your application doesn't seem to need a prime number finder or a bowling score calculator. It needs you to add lines of code to existing methods or new methods to existing classes. It doesn't really seem to need new classes, so the initial momentum and resolution you've built to go and be a unit tester fizzles anticlimactically when you stare at your code base.

What's going on here?

Recognizing Inhospitable Terrain

The first thing to understand is that your code base probably wasn't written with testability in mind. There's nothing wrong with you for not being able to see where unit testing fits in, because it doesn't. In the last chapter, I talked about things you'll see that will torpedo your efforts to test a particular method or piece of code, but let me speak to some entire architectures and patterns that don't lend themselves to testability. It's not that code written with these technologies and patterns *can't* be tested – it's just that it won't be easy for you.

1. <u>Active Record</u> as an architectural pattern. This is a pattern in which you create classes that are in-memory representations of database tables, views or stored procedures. If you see in your code base a class called "Customer" that has methods like "GetById()", "Up-

date()" and "MoveNext()," you've got yourself an Active Record architecture. This architecture tightly couples your database to your domain logic and your domain logic to the rules for navigating through domain objects. You can't test any of these objects since any operation you perform on them sends them scurrying off to create database connections and parameterized queries and all manner of other untestable stuff. And since decomposition and decoupling is the path toward unit testing, this sort of tight coupling of everything in your code is the path away from it.

2.   WinForms. WinForms in the .NET world are tried and true when it comes to rapidly cranking out functional little applications, but you have to work really, really hard to make code that uses them testable. Q&A sites are littered with people trying to understand how to make WinForms testable, which should tell you that making them testable is not trivial. If you have WinForms and Active Record both in the same code base, at least the architecture is split into two concerns. But it's split into two thoroughly untestable ones.

3.   Web Forms. See WinForms. Web Forms is very similar in terms of framework testability, and for pretty similar reasons. Web Forms is arguably even harder to test, however, because it's predicated on spewing out reams and reams of HTML, CSS and JavaScript while allowing you to pretend you're writing a desktop app. I've talked about my opinion of this technology before.

4.   Wizard/markup-reliant code. Do you use the Web Forms grid wizard thing to generate your grids? Do you define object data sources, such as DB connections or files, in the markup? Practices like these are the epitome of quick and dirty, rapid-prototyping implementations that hopelessly cross couple your ap-

plications beyond all testability. If this is something that's done in your group/code base, testing is basically a non-starter until you go in a different architectural direction.

5. Everything in your application is in a user control/form. I've seen this called "Smart UI" and it basically means that there's absolutely no separation of concerns in your code. The UI elements create database connections, write to files, implement business rules – they do everything. Code like this is impossible to unit test.

If any of this is sounding familiar, your task might be daunting. I have my own preferences, but I'm trying not to offer a value judgment here as much as I'm letting you know what you're up against. I'm like a mortgage broker that's saying to you, "If you want to own a home, that's a great goal. But if you are eight months behind on your rent and have no personal savings, you're going to have some work to do first." If I've described your code base in the list above, you face different challenges than a green field developer. And since you've presumably been contributing to these code bases, you're probably very used to implementation techniques that don't result in testable code. You're going to need to change your thinking and your coding practices in order to start writing testable code.

Once we've discussed how to get you writing testable code, I'll come back to these macroscopic concerns and give some pointers for how to improve the situation. But, for now, on to a revised approach to coding. The following holds true whether you're banging away at some legacy WinForms/Active Record application or starting a brand new MVC 4 site.

Add New Methods and Classes First, Ask Questions Later

First thing to abide by is to favor adding new things to the code over modifying existing things in the code. You may have heard this before in the context of the "Open/Closed Principle," but that's a

guide for how to write your classes. (Basically, it ad̶
to write classes that others can extend and overrid̶
change.) I'm talking about how to deal with existing code bases. ᴛ᷄
put it simply and bluntly, it's a lot easier to both code and test brand
spankin' new classes than to write and test changes to existing ones.
We all know this. It's at the heart of why we as developers always
lean toward rewriting others' code instead of understanding and
working with it.

Now, this might not win you friends. In shops where people
tend to write procedural code (you know, the kind you're trying
to get away from writing), they seem to have some <u>weird fear of
creating too many classes</u> and <u>masochistic attachment to monolithic
structures</u>. You might have to compromise or practice on your
own if you run afoul of the project's architect, but the exercise is
invaluable. It's going to propel you toward decoupling as a default
rather than an exception. Doing new things? Time for a new class
and some unit tests.

I know what you're thinking: "But what if the thing that needs to
be done has to be done in the middle of some method somewhere?"
Well, instantiate your new class at that point and use it. "But what
if it needs a bunch of fields from the class it's in and variables from
the method?" Pass them in through the constructor or method call.
"But won't that make my design bad?" It already is bad, but at least
now you're making part of it testable. When your code is testable
and under test, everything is easier to fix later.

You'll have to use some discretion, obviously, but shift your
attitude here. Don't look at a project that has nothing but .aspx files
and their code behind and hide classes in there for fear of breaking
with tradition. Boldly add pure .cs files to the code base. Add unit
tests for those .cs files you're creating. (Apologies to Java readers,
but this has no real Java equivalent that I can think of having used.
Plus, the Java stack in general seems not to have the same level of
untestable cruft built into frameworks.) It's a lot harder for someone,
even the project architect, to give you a hard time if your new way of
doing things is covered by unit tests. Even if they're hostile <u>expert
beginners</u>, they're hard pressed not to sound silly if they say, "we

don't do that here." You'll at least have a better chance of pushing this change through with the unit tests than without them.

Ask Questions in the Right Order: What, How, When

Now that you're creating a lot of new classes and instantiating them in the old untestable ones, it's time to start working on what kind of code you write. If you've practiced and come back, I suspect that you're starting to be able to write a few useful tests but are perhaps still struggling. And I bet it's because the line between where the old class ends and your new one begins is a little hazy. Maybe they share some common fields. Maybe when you instantiate the class you're testing, you hand it a "this" reference so that it can go picking through the properties on the untestable behemoth from which you're escaping. This is the next thing we need to tighten up – stop doing that. A clear, concise division of labor between the classes is necessary, and it's not possible if they share all of the same fields, properties, state, etc. That's like a breakup where you two continue to live together, share a car, and go to the movies on weekends.

The best way to achieve this clean split is with good abstraction, and the best way to do *that* is to remember "what, how, when." When it's time to change the code base, remember that you want to favor creating a new class. But before you do that, ask yourself "what?" while avoiding the other two questions. What should I name this class? What should it do? What should it expose as its public methods? Don't start thinking about *how* those methods or classes should work, and especially don't start thinking about *when* anything at all should happen – just think about what. Give it a good name that defines a clear purpose, and then give it a good set of methods and properties that draw attention to why it's a different concept than the class that will be using it. Ask yourself what the boundaries between the two classes will be so that you can minimize the amount of shared information. And now, start stubbing out those methods with no implementation and start stubbing out some test methods with names that say what the methods will do. At this point, you're ready for "how." Start actually implementing the "what" and testing that your implementation works in the unit tests. Believe me, it's much, much easier to implement methods this way. If you think about "what" and "how" at the same time, you start writing confusing code, and not even you have faith in when you're done. Implementation alone is much easier when you have a clear picture of "what," and unit testing is a breeze.

Once everything is implemented, you can start thinking about "when." When should you instantiate the class, and when should you call its methods? But don't spend too much time with "when" in your head because it's dangerous. Does that sound weird? Let me explain.

"When Code" is Monolithic Code

Picture two methods. One is a 700-line juggernaut with more control flow statements than you can keep track of without a spreadsheet. The other is five lines long, consisting only of an initialize statement, a foreach, and a return statement. With which would you rather work? I imagine the response is unanimous here. Even if you tend to crank out these kinds of large methods, when you step through the debugger, looking for the cause of a bug and finding yourself in some huge method, your heart sinks and you settle in with snacks and caffeine because it's going to be a long day.

Now with these two methods in mind, imagine if we were pair programming together and I simply asked "when?" With the tiny method, you'd probably say, "What do you mean by 'when' – I mean, you initialize before the loop and you return when you find the record you're looking for. What a weird question!" With the other method, you'd probably affect a thousand-yard stare and say, "Man, I don't even know where to begin." The answer to that question would fill pages. Books. Because you set the first loop counter j equal to the third loop counter k about 20 lines before the fourth try-catch and 15 lines before you set the middle loop counter j equal to four. Unless, of course, you threw that exception up on line 2090, in which case j might never have been initialized. Er, wait, I think that happened somewhere near the fifth while loop in that else condition up there. Oh, there's so much "when," but it's all slammed together in a method that won't allow you to test any of it. Lots of thinking about "when" breeds huge methods like a Petri dish of bacteria.

"When" code is procedural at its core, and procedural "when" code is an anathema to object-oriented unit testing, which is all about "what" and "how." Remember earlier in the book when I said that multi-threaded code was really, really hard to test? Well, that's just a subset of an idea called "temporal coupling," and what we're talking about here also falls under that umbrella. Temporal coupling is what happens when things have to be executed in a specific order or else they do not work.

Imagine that you're coding up a model for someone's day. When you think of how to do this, do you think, "first he gets up, then he brushes his teeth, then he showers, then he puts on his clothes, then... then he comes home, then he eats dinner, then he watches TV, then he goes to bed?" Do you code this up with constructs like this:

```
1   public void GoAboutMyDay()
2   {
3       bool wokeUp = WakeUp();
4       if (wokeUp == true)
5       {
6           bool showered = Shower();
7           if (showered == true)
8           {
9               bool putOnClothes = PutOnClothes();
10              if(putOnClothes)
11                  //You get the idea
12          }
13      }
14  }
```

This method is all about "when." It's entirely procedural, and it's going to be horrifying when it's complete. When you get into the fortieth nested if condition, maybe someone will come along and flatten it out with a bunch of inverted early returns. Or maybe not, because maybe some of if clauses start sprouting else conditions with loops in them. And maybe the methods being called start communicating with one another via boolean flag fields in the class. Who knows – this thing is on the precipice of becoming unstoppable. It might just achieve sentience at some point, so that when you try to start deleting conditionals, it says, "I can't let you do that, Dave," and puts them back.

The root problem behind it all is the "when" and the procedural thinking because you're orienting the implementation around the order of the activities rather than the nature of the activities. Unit testing is all about deconstructing things into their smallest possible chunks and asserting things about those chunks. Temporal coupling and "when" logic is all about chaining and fusing things together.

If you were thinking about "what" first here, you would form a much different mental model of a person's day. You'd say things to yourself like, "well, during the course of a person's day, he probably wakes up, gets dressed, eats breakfast – well, actually eats one or more meals – maybe works if it's a weekday, goes to bed at some point," etc. Whereas in the procedural "when" modeling you were necessarily building a juggernaut method, here you're dreaming up the names of methods and/or classes that can be unit tested separately and in isolation. It's no reach to say, "okay, let's have a Meal class that will have the following methods…"

Only at the end will you decide "when." You'll decide it after you've stubbed things out with the "what" and implemented/unit tested them with the "how." "When" is a detail that you should allow yourself to figure out at any point down the line. If you nail down what and how, you will have testable, modular and manageable code as you create your classes.

Other Design Considerations for Your New Classes

I'll wrap up here with a few additional tips for creating testable designs when adding code to your code bases:

1. Avoid using fields to communicate between your methods by setting flags and tracking state. Favor having methods that can be executed at any time and in any order.

2. Don't instantiate things in your constructor. Favor passing them in. (We'll talk about this in detail in a future chapter.)

3. Similarly, don't have a lot of code or do a lot of work in your constructor. This will make your class painful to setup for test.

4. In your methods, accept parameters that are as decomposed as possible. For instance, don't accept a Customer object if all you do with it is read its SSN property. In that case, just ask for the SSN.

5. Avoid writing public static methods. These are easy enough to test (often), but they start introducing testability problems when you write code that uses them. (This might be hard to swallow at first, but mull over the idea of simply not using static methods anymore.)

6. The earlier you start writing your unit tests, the better. If you find that you're having a hard time testing your new code, it's more likely a problem with the code than with unit testing it, and if you write tests early, you'll discover these problems before you get too far and fix them.

This chapter has covered ways to write unit tests "from here forward" and ways to stop adding untested code to code bases. In the next chapter, I'll talk about how to start getting the legacy code under test.

Addendum: Mitigating the Hostile Test Environments

Finally, as promised, here are ways to accommodate testing in the less-than-ideal architectures mentioned above, if you're curious or want to do some more research:

Instead of Active Record, look at some kind of ORM solution like NHibernate or Entity Framework. These are tools that generate all of the code for you to access the database so that you don't have to worry about testing that code and you can focus on writing only your (testable) domain code. Barring that, try to separate the three concerns of Active Record objects: modeling the database, connecting to the database, and modeling a domain object. The first concern adds no value, and the second two can be broken out into separate objects where the only thing hard to test is the actual database access.

Instead of WinForms, favor WPF when possible. If that isn't possible, see if you can use the Model-View-Presenter (MVP) pattern to move as much logic out of the untestable code-behind as possible.

To be blunt, from a testing/decoupling perspective, Web Forms is a disaster. You can have some limited success by adopting a more passive binding model and moving as much code out of the code-behind as possible, but it's all pretty awkward. Web Forms really seems more about rapid-prototyping and Microsoft-Accessing web development than producing scalable, sophisticated architectures. If you're using wizards to generate your application's architecture, cut it out. If you're defining implementation details in markup, cut it out. Markup is for layout, not unit-testable business logic or state logic. If you depend on definitions in markup to drive your application's behavior, you're relying exorbitantly on a third-party framework, which is always extremely brittle from a testability perspective.

To fix Smart UI, you just have to factor toward a more decoupled architecture. Start pulling different concerns out of the user controls and forms and finding a home for them.

CHAPTER 5

INVADING LEGACY CODE IN THE NAME OF TESTABILITY

I f, in the movie Braveheart, the Scots had been battling a nasty legacy code base instead of the English under Edward Longshanks, the conversation after the battle at Stirling between Wallace and minor Scottish noble MacClannough might have gone like this:

Wallace:	We have prevented new bugs in the code base by adding new unit tests for all new code, but bugs will still happen.
MacClannough:	What will you do?
Wallace:	I will invade the legacy code, and defeat the bugs on their own ground.

MacClannough (snorts in disbelief): Invade? That's impossible.

Wallace: Why? Why is that impossible? You're so concerned with squabbling over the best process for handling endless defects that you've missed your God-given right to something better.

Goofy as the introduction to this chapter may be, there's a point here: while unit testing brand new classes that you add to the code base is a victory and brings benefit, to reap the real game-changing rewards you have to be a bit of a rabble-rouser. You can't just leave that festering mass of legacy code as it is, or it will generate defects even without you touching it. Others may scoff or even outright oppose your efforts, but you've got to get that legacy code under test at some point or it will dominate your project and give you unending headaches.

So far in this book, I've covered the basics of unit testing, when to do it, and when it might be too daunting. Most recently,

I talked about how to design new code to make it testable. Now, I'm going to talk about how to wrangle your existing mess to start making *it* testable.

Easy Does It

A quick word of caution here before going any further: don't try to do too much all at once. Your first task after reading the rest of this chapter should be selecting something small in your code base to try it on if you want to target production and get it approved by an architect or lead, if that's required. Another option is just to create a playpen version of your code base to throw away and thus earn yourself a bit more latitude, but either way, I'd advise small, manageable stabs before really bearing down. What specifically you try to do is up to you, but I think it's worth proceeding slowly and steadily. I'm all about incremental improvement in things that I do.

Also, at the end of this chapter I'll offer some further reading that I highly recommend. And, in fact, I recommend reading it before or as you get started moving your legacy code toward testability. These books will be a great help and will delve much further into the subjects that I'll cover here.

Test What You Can

Perhaps this goes without saying, but let's just say it anyway to be thorough. There will be stuff in the legacy code base you can test. You'll find the odd class with few dependencies or a method dangling off somewhere that, for a refreshing change, doesn't reference some giant singleton. So your first task there is writing tests for that code.

But there's a way to do this and a way not to do this. The way to do it is to write what's known as <u>characterization tests</u> that simply document the behavior of the existing system. The way not to do this is to introduce 'corrections' and cleanup as you go. The linked blog post goes into more detail, but suffice it to say that modifying untested legacy code is like playing Jenga — you never really know ahead of time which brick removal is going to cause an avalanche of problems. That's why legacy code is so hard to change and so unpleasant to work with. Adding tests is like adding little warnings that say, "dude, not that brick!!!" So while the tower may be faulty and leaning and of shoddy construction, it *is* standing. You don't want to go changing things without putting your warning system in place.

So, long story short, don't modify — just write tests. Even if a method tells you that it adds two integers and what it really does is divide one by the other, just write a passing test for it. Do not 'fix' it (that'll come later when your tests help you understand the system and renaming the method is a more attractive option). Iterate through your code base and do it everywhere you can. If you can instantiate the class to get to the method you want to test and then write asserts about it (bearing in mind the testability problems I've covered, like GUI, static state, threading, etc.), do it. Move on to the next step once you've done the simple stuff everywhere. After all, this is easy practice, and practice helps.

Go Searching for Extractable Code

Now that you have a pretty good handle on writing testable code as you're adding it to the code base, as well as experience getting untested but testable code under test, it's time to start chipping away at the rest. One of the easiest ways to do this is to hunt down methods in your code base that you can't test but not because of the contents in them. Here are two examples that come to mind:

| 1<br>2<br>3<br>4<br>5<br>6<br>7<br>8<br>9<br>10<br>11<br>12<br>13<br>14<br>15<br>16<br>17<br>18<br>19<br>20<br>21<br>22<br>23<br>24<br>25 | ```csharp
public class Untestable1
{
    public Untestable1()
    {
                    TestabilityKiller.Instance.
DoSomethingHorribleWithGlobalVariables();
    }

    public int AddTwoNumbers(int x, int y)
    {
        return x + y;
    }
}

public class Untestable2
{
    public void PerformSomeBusinessLogic(Custo
merOrder order)
    {
                Console.WriteLine("Total is " +
AddTwoNumbers(order.Subtotal, order.Tax));
    }

    private int AddTwoNumbers(int x, int y)
    {
        return x + y;
    }
}
``` |

The first class is untestable because you can't instantiate it without kicking off global state modification and who knows what else. But the AddTwoNumbers method is imminently testable if you could remove that roadblock. In the second example, the AddTwoNumbers method is testable once again, in theory, but with a roadblock: it's not public.
```

In both cases, we have a simple solution: move the method somewhere else. Let's put it into a class called "BasicArithmeticPerformer" as shown below. I do realize that there are other solutions to make these methods testable, but we'll talk about them later. And I'll tell you what I consider to be a terrible solution to one of the testability issues that I'll talk about now: making the private method public or rigging up your test runner with gimmicks to allow testing of private methods. You're creating an observer effect with testing when you do this — altering the way the code would look so that you can test it. Don't compromise your encapsulation design to make things testable. If you find yourself wanting to test what's going on in private methods, that's a strong, strong indicator that you're trying to test the wrong thing or that you have a design flaw.

```
1    public class BasicArithmeticPerformer
2    {
3        public int AddTwoNumbers(int x, int y)
4        {
5            return x + y;
6        }
7    }
```

Now *that's* a testable class. So what do the other classes now look like?

| 1<br>2<br>3<br>4<br>5<br>6<br>7<br>8<br>9<br>10<br>11<br>12<br>13<br>14<br>15<br>16<br>17<br>18<br>19<br>20<br>21<br>22<br>23<br>24<br>25 | ```csharp
public class Untestable1
{
    public Untestable1()
    {
        TestabilityKiller.Instance.DoSomethingHorribleWithGlobalVariables();
    }

    private int AddTwoNumbers(int x, int y)
    {
        return new BasicArithmeticPerformer().AddTwoNumbers(x, y);
    }
}

public class Untestable2
{
    public void PerformSomeBusinessLogic(CustomerOrder order)
    {
        Console.WriteLine("Total is " + AddTwoNumbers(order.Subtotal, order.Tax));
    }

    public int AddTwoNumbers(int x, int y)
    {
        return new BasicArithmeticPerformer().AddTwoNumbers(x, y);
    }
}
``` |

Yep, it's that simple. In fact, it has to be that simple. Modifying this untestable legacy code is like walking a high wire without a safety net, so you have to change as little as possible. Extracting a method to another class is very low risk as far as refactorings go since the most likely problem to occur (particularly if using an automated
```

tool) is non-compiling. There's always a risk, but getting legacy code under test is lower risk in the long run than allowing it to continue rotting, and the risk of this particular approach is minimal.

On the other side of things, is this a significant win? I would say so. Even ignoring the eliminated duplication, you now have gone from 0 test coverage to 50% in these classes. Test coverage is not a goal in and of itself, but you can now rest a little easier knowing that you have a change warning system in place for half of your code. If someone comes along later and says, "Oh, I'll just change that plus to a minus so that I can 'reuse' this method for my purposes," you'll have something in place that will throw up a bid red X and say, "Hey, you're breaking things!" And besides, Rome wasn't built in a day — you're going to be going through your code base building up a test suite one action like this at a time.

Code that refers to no class fields is easy when it comes to extracting functionality to a safe, testable location. But what if there is instance-level state in the mix? For example...

```
1   public class Untestable3
1   {
2       int _someField;
3
4       public Untestable3()
5       {
6                       TestabilityKiller.Instance.
7   DoSomethingHorribleWithGlobalVariables();
8           _someField = TestabilityKiller.Instance.
9   GetSomeGlobalVariableValue();
10      }
11
12      public int AddToGlobal(int x)
13      {
14          return x + _someField;
15      }
    }
```

That's a little tougher because we can't just pull _someField into a new, testable class. But what if we made a quick change that got us onto more familiar ground? Such as...

```
     public class Untestable3
1    {
2        int _someField;
3
4        public Untestable3()
5        {
6                        TestabilityKiller.Instance.
7    DoSomethingHorribleWithGlobalVariables();
8                _someField = TestabilityKiller.Instance.
9    GetSomeGlobalVariableValue();
10       }
11
12       public int AddToGlobal(int x)
13       {
14           return AddTwoNumbers(x, _someField);
15       }
16
17       private int AddTwoNumbers(int x, int y)
18       {
19           return x + y;
20       }
     }
```

Aha! This looks familiar, and I think we know how to get a testable method out of this thing now. In general, when you have class fields or local variables, those are going to become arguments to methods and/or constructors of the new, testable class that you're creating and instantiating. Understand going in that the more local variables and class fields you have to deal with, the more of a testing headache the thing you're extracting is going to be. As you go, you'll learn to look for code in legacy classes that refers to comparably few local variables and especially fields in the current class as a refactoring target, but this is an acquired knack.

The reason this is not especially trivial is that we're nibbling here at an idea in static analysis of object-oriented programs called "cohesion." Cohesion, explained informally, is the idea that units of code that you find together belong together. For example, a Car class with an instance field called Engine and three methods, StartEngine(), StopEngine( )and RestartEngine(), is highly cohesive. All of its methods operate on its field. A class called Car that has an Engine field and a Dishwasher field and two methods, StartEngine() and EmptyDiswasher(), is not cohesive. When you go sniping for testable code that you can move to other classes, what you're really looking for is low-cohesion additions to existing classes. Perhaps some class has a method that refers to no instance variables, meaning you could really put it anywhere. Or perhaps you find a class with three methods that refer to a single instance variable that none of the other 40 methods in a class refer to because they all use some other fields on the class. Those three methods and the field they use could definitely go in another class that you could make testable.

When refactoring toward testability, non-cohesive code is the low-hanging fruit that you're looking for. If it seems strange that poorly designed code (and non-cohesive code is a characteristic of poor design) offers ripe refactoring opportunities, we're just making lemonade out of lemons. The fact that someone slammed unrelated pieces of code together to create a franken-class just means that you're going to have that much easier of a time pulling them apart.

Realize that Giant Methods are Begging to be Classes

It's getting less and less common these days, but do you ever see object-oriented code and are able to tell that the author meandered his way over from writing C back in the one-pass compiler days? If you don't know what I mean, it's code that has this sort of form:

1	public void PerformSomeBusinessLogic(Customer Order order)
2	{
3	int x, y, z;
4	double a, b, c;
5	int counter;
6	CustomerOrder tempOrder;
7	int secondLoopCounter;
8	string output;
9	string firstTimeInput;
10	
11	//Alright, now let›s get started because this is
12	going to be looooonnnng method...
13	...
	}

C programmers wrote code like this because in old standards of C it was necessary to declare variables right after the opening brace of a scope before you started doing things like assignment and control flow statements. They've carried it forward over the years because, well, old habits die hard. Interestingly, they're actually doing you a favor. Here's why.

When looking at a method like this, you know you're in for doozy. If it has this many local variables, it's going to be long, convoluted and painful. In the C# world, it probably has regions in it that divide up the different responsibilities of the method. This is also a problem but a lemons-to-lemonade opportunity for us. These C-style programmers are actually telling you how to turn their giant, unwieldy method into a class. All of those variables at the top? Those are your class fields. All of those regions (or comments in languages that don't support regioning)? Method names.

In one of the resources I'll recommend, "Uncle" Bob Martin said something along the lines of "large methods are where classes go to hide." What this means is that when you encounter some gigantic method that spans dozens or hundreds of lines, what you really have is something that should be a class. It's functionality that has grown too big for a method. So what do you do? Well, you create a new class with its local variables as fields, its region names/comments as method titles, and class fields as dependencies. Then you delegate the responsibility.

```
1   public class Untestable4
2   {
3       public void PerformSomeBusinessLogic(Custom
4   erOrder order)
5       {
6           var extractedClass = new MaybeTestable();
7           extractedClass.Region1Title();
8           extractedClass.Region2Title();
9           extractedClass.Region3Title();
10      }
11  }
12
13  public class MaybeTestable
14  {
15      int x, y, z;
16      double a, b, c;
17      int counter;
18      CustomerOrder tempOrder;
19      int secondLoopCounter;
20      string output;
21      string firstTimeInput;
22
23      public void Region1Title()
24      {
25  ...
```

In this example, there are no fields in the untestable class that the method is using. But if there were, one way to handle this is to pass them into the constructor of the extracted class and have them as fields there as well. So, assuming this extraction goes smoothly (and it might not be that easy if the giant method has a lot of temporal coupling, resulting from, say, recycled variables),

what is gained here? Well, first of all, you've slain a giant m.
which will inevitably be good from a design perspective. But wh..
about testability?

In this case, it's possible that you still won't have testable
methods, but it's likely that you will. The original gigantic method
wasn't testable. They never are. There's really way too much going on
in them for meaningful testing to occur — too many control flow
statements, loops, global variables, file I/O, etc. Giant methods are
giant because they do a lot of things, and if you do enough code
things, you're going to start running over the bounds of testability.
But the new methods are going to be split up and more focused and
there's a good chance that at least one of them will be testable in
a meaningful way. Plus, with the extracted class, you have control
over the new constructor that you're creating whereas you didn't
with the legacy class. So you can ensure that the class can at least be
instantiated. At the end of the day, you're improving the design and
introducing a seam that you can get at for testing.

Ask for Your Dependencies — Don't Declare Them

Another change you can make that may be relatively
straightforward is to move dependencies out of the scope of your
class — especially icky dependencies. Take a look at the original
version of Untestable3 again.

```
1    public class Untestable3
2    {
3        int _someField;
4
5        public Untestable3()
6        {
7            TestabilityKiller.Instance.DoSomethingHorribleWithGlobalVariables();
8            _someField = TestabilityKiller.Instance.GetSomeGlobalVariableValue();
9        }
10
11
12       public int AddToGlobal(int x)
13       {
14           return x + _someField;
15       }
    }
```

When instantiated, this class goes and rattles some global state cages, doing God-knows-what (icky), and then retrieves something from global state (icky). We want to get a test around the AddToGlobal method, but we can't instantiate this class. For all we know, to get the value of "someField" the singleton gets the British Prime Minster on the phone and asks him for a random number between 1 and 1000 — and we can't automate that in a test suite. Now, the earlier option of extracting code is, of course, viable, but we also have the option of punting the offending code out of this class. (This may or may not be practical depending on where and how this class is used, but let's assume it is). Say there's only one client of this code:

```
1    public class Untestable3Client
2    {
3        public void SomeMethod()
4        {
5            var untestable = new Untestable3();
6            untestable.AddToGlobal(12);
7        }
8    }
```

All we really want out of the constructor is a value for "_someField". All of that stuff with the singleton is just noise. Because of the nature of global variables, we can do the stuff Untestable3's constructor was doing anywhere. So what about this as an alternative?

```
1      public class Untestable3Client
2      {
3          public void SomeMethod()
4          {
5              TestabilityKiller.Instance.
6  DoSomethingHorribleWithGlobalVariables();
7              var someField = TestabilityKiller.Instance.
8  GetSomeGlobalVariableValue();
9              var untestable = new Untestable3(someField);
10             untestable.AddToGlobal(12);
11         }
12     }
13
14     public class Untestable3
15     {
16         int _someField;
17
18         public Untestable3(int someField)
19         {
20             _someField = someField;
21         }
22
23         public int AddToGlobal(int x)
24         {
25             return x + _someField;
26         }
27     }
```

This new code is going to do the same thing as the old code, but with one important difference: Untestable3 is now a liar. It's a liar because it's testable. There's nothing about global state in there at all. It just takes an integer and stores it, which is no problem to test. You're an old pro by now at unit testing that's this easy.

When it comes to testability, the new operator and global state are your enemies. If you have code that makes use of these things, you need to punt. Punt those things out of your code by doing what we did here: executing voids before your constructors/methods are called and asking for things returned from global state or new in your constructors/methods. This is another pretty low-impact way of altering a given class to make it testable, particularly when the only problem is that a class is instantiating untestable classes or reaching out into the global state.

Ruthlessly Eliminate Law of Demeter Violations

If you're not familiar with the idea, the <u>Law of Demeter</u>, or Principle of Least Knowledge, basically demands that methods refer to as few object instances as possible in order to do their work. You can look at the link for more specifics on what exactly this law says and what exactly is and is not a violation, but the most common form you'll see is strings of dots (or arrows in C++) where you're walking an object graph: Property.NestedProperty. NestedNestedProperty.You.Get.The.Idea. (It is worth mentioning that the existence of multiple dots is not always a violation of the Law of Demeter — <u>fluent interfaces</u> in general and Linq in the C# world specifically are counterexamples). It's when you're given some object instance and you go picking through its innards to find what you're looking for.

One of the most immediately memorable ways of thinking about why this is problematic is to consider what happens when you're at the grocery store buying groceries. When the clerk tells you that the total is $86.28, you swipe your Visa. What you don't do is wordlessly hand him your wallet. What you definitely don't do is take off your pants and hand those over so that he can find your wallet. Consider the following code, bearing in mind that example:

```
   public class HardToTest
1  {
2                              public          string
3  PrepareSsnMessage(CustomerOrder order)
4      {
5          return «Social Security number is « + order.
6  Customer.PersonalInfo.Ssn;
7      }
   }
```

The method in this class just prepends an explanatory string to a social security number. So why on earth do I need something called a customer order? That's crazy — as crazy as handing the store clerk your pants. And from a testing perspective, this is a real headache. In order to test this method, I have to create a customer, then create an order and hand that to the customer, then create a personal info object and hand that to the customer's order, and then create an SSN and hand that to the customer's order's personal info. And that's if everything goes well. What if one of those classes — say, Customer — invokes a singleton in its constructor. Well, now I can't test the "PrepareSsnMessage" in HardToTest because the Customer class uses a singleton. That's absolutely insane.

Let's try this instead:

1	public class HardToTest
2	{
3	public string PrepareSsnMessage(string ssn)
4	{
5	return «Social Security number is « + ssn;
6	}
7	}

Ah, now that's easy to test. And we can test it even if the Customer class is doing weird, untestable things because those things aren't our problem. What about clients, though? They're used to passing customer orders in, not SSNs. Well, tough — we're making this class testable. They know about customer order and its SSN, so let them incur the Law of Demeter violation and figure out how to clean it up. You can only make your code testable one class at a time. That class and its Law of Demeter violation is tomorrow's project.

When it comes to testing, the more stuff your code knows about, the more setup and potential problems you have. If you don't test your code, it's easy to write train wrecks like the "before" method in this section without really considering the ramifications of what you're doing. The unit tests force you to think about it — "man, this method is a huge hassle to test because problems in classes I don't even care about are preventing me from testing!" Guess what. That's a design smell. Problems in weird classes you don't care about aren't just impacting your tests — they're also impacting your class under test, in production, when things go wrong and when you're trying to debug.

Understand the Significance of Polymorphism for Testing

I'll leave off with a segue into the next chapter, which is going to be about a concept called "test doubles." I will explain that concept then and address a significant barrier that you're probably starting to bump into in your testing travels. But that isn't my purpose here.

For now I'll just say that you should understand the attraction of using polymorphic code for testing.

Consider the following code:

```
   public class Customer
   {
1      public  string  FirstName  {  get
2  {     return            TestabilityKiller.Instance.
3  GoGetCustomerFirstNameFromTheDatabase(); } }
4  }
5
6  public class CustomerPropertyFormatter
7  {
8      public string PrepareFirstNameMessage(Custom
9  er customer)
10     {
11         return «Customer first name is « + customer.
12  FirstName;
       }
   }
```

Here you have a class, CustomerPropertyFormatter, that should be pretty easy to test. I mean, it just takes a customer and accesses some string property on it for formatting purposes. But when you actually write a test for this, everything goes wrong. You create a customer to give to your method and your test blows up because of singletons and databases and whatnot. You can write a test with a null argument and amend this code to handle null gracefully, but that's about it.

But never fear — polymorphism to the rescue. If you make a relatively small modification to the Customer class, you set yourself up nicely. All you have to do is make the FirstName property virtual. Once you've done that, here's a unit test that you can write:

```
       public class DummyCustomer : Customer
       {
1          private string _firstName;
2          public override string FirstName { get { return
3      _firstName; } }
4
5          /// <summary>
6              /// Initializes a new instance of the
7      DummyCustomer class.
8          /// </summary>
9          public DummyCustomer(string firstName)
10         {
11             _firstName = firstName;
12         }
13     }
14
15         [TestMethod,                    Owner("ebd"),
16     TestCategory("Proven"), TestCategory("Unit")]
17         public void Adds_Text_To_FirstName()
18         {
19             string firstName = "Erik";
20             var customer = new DummyCustomer(firstName);
21             var formatter = new CustomerPropertyFormatter();
22
23             Assert.IsTrue(formatter.PrepareFirstNameMe
       ssage(customer).Contains(firstName));
       }
```

Notice that there is a class, DummyCustomer declared inside of the test class that inherits from the Customer class. DummyCustomer is an example of a test double. You'll notice that I've created a scenario here where I define a benign version of FirstName that I can control. I effectively bypass that database-singleton thing and create a version of the class that exists only in the test project and allows me to substitute a simple, friendly value that I can test against.

As I said, I'll dive much more into test doubles in the next chapter, but for the time being, understand the power of polymorphism for testability. If the legacy code has methods in it that are hard to use, you can create much more testable situations by the use of interface implementation, inheritance and the virtual keyword. Conversely, you can make testing a nightmare by using keywords like "final" and "sealed" (Java and C#, respectively). There are valid reasons to use these, but if you want a testable code base, you should favor liberal support of inheritance and interface implementation.

A Note of Caution

In the sections above, I've talked about refactorings that you can do on legacy code bases and mentioned that there is some risk associated with doing so. It is up to you to assess the level of risk of touching your legacy code, but know that any changes you make to legacy code without first instrumenting unit tests can be breaking changes, even small ones guided by automated refactoring tools. There are ways to 'cheat' and tips and techniques to get a method under test before you refactor it, such as temporarily making private fields public or local variables into public fields. The Michael Feathers book below talks extensively about these techniques to truly minimize the risk.

The techniques that I'm suggesting here would be ones that I'd typically undertake when requirements changes or bugs were forcing me to make a bunch of changes to the legacy code anyway, and the business understood and was willing to undertake the risk of changing it. I tend to refactor opportunistically like that. What you do is really up to your discretion, but I don't want to be responsible for you doing some rogue refactoring and torpedoing your production code because you thought it was safe. Changing untested legacy code is never safe, and it's important for you to understand the risks.

More Information

As mentioned earlier, here are some excellent resources for more information on working with and testing legacy code bases:

- Working Effectively with Legacy Code by Michael Feathers

- Clean Code by Robert (Uncle Bob) Martin

- Clean Coders video series, by Robert Martin

The Art of Unit Testing by Roy Osherove (I have not personally read this, but I respect his work that I'm familiar with and have seen it recommended)

CHAPTER 6

TEST DOUBLES

I n the last two chapters, I talked about how to test new code in your code base and then how to bring your legacy code under test. Toward the end of the last chapter, I talked a bit about the concept of test doubles. The example I showed was one in which I used polymorphism to create a "dummy" class that I used in a test to circumvent otherwise untestable code. Here, I'll dive into a lot more detail on the subject, starting out with a much simpler example than that and building to a more sophisticated way to handle the management of your test doubles.

First, a Bit of Theory

Before we get into test doubles, however, let's stop and talk about what we're actually doing, including theory about unit tests. So far, I've showed a lot of examples of unit tests and talked about what they look like and how they work (for instance, in chapter two where I talk about Arrange, Act, Assert). But what I haven't addressed, specifically, is how the test code should interact with the production code. So let's talk about that a bit now.

By far the most common case when unit testing is that you instantiate a class under test in the "arrange" part of your unit test, and then you do whatever additional setup is necessary before calling some method on that class. Then you assert something that should have happened as a result of that method call. Let's return to the example of prime finder from earlier and look at a simple test:

1	[TestMethod]
2	public void Returns_False_For_One()
3	{
4	var primeFinder = new PrimeFinder(); //Arrange
5	
6	bool result = primeFinder.IsPrime(1); //Act
7	
8	Assert.IsFalse(result); //Assert
9	}

This should be reviewed from the perspective of Arrange, Act, Assert, but let's look specifically at the "act" line. Here is the real crux of the test. We're writing tests about the IsPrime method and this is where the action happens. In this line of code, we give the method an input and record its output, so it's the perfect microcosm for what I'm going to discuss about a class under test: its interactions with other objects. You see, unit testing isn't about executing your code — you can do that with integration tests, console apps, or even just by running the application. Unit testing, at its core, is about isolating your classes and running experiments on them, as if you were a scientist in a lab. And this means controlling all of the inputs to your class — stimulus, if you will — so that you can observe what it puts out.

Controlling the inputs in the PrimeFinder class is simple. There are no invocations of global/static state (which will become an important theme as we proceed). You can see by looking at the unit test that the only input to the class under test (CUT) is the integer 1. This means that the only input/stimulus that we supply to the class is a simple integer, making it quite easy to make assertions about its behavior. Generally speaking, the simpler the inputs to a class, the easier that class is to test.

There are Inputs and There are Inputs

Omitting certain edge cases I can think of (and probably some that I'm not thinking of), let's consider a handful of relatively straightforward ways that a class might get ahold of input information. There is what I did above — passing it into a method. Another common way to give information to a class is to use constructor parameters or setter methods/properties. I'll refer to these as "passive collaboration" from the perspective of the CUT, since it's simply being given the things that it needs. There is also what I'll call "semi-passive collaboration," which describes passing a dependency to the CUT and the CUT interacting in great detail with that dependency, mutating its state and querying it. An example of this would be "Car theCar = new Car(new Engine())", in which performing operations on Car related to starting and driving result in rather elaborate modifications to the state of Engine. It's still passive in the sense that you're handing the engine class to the car, but it's not as passive as simply handing it an integer. In general, passive input is input that the scope instantiating the CUT controls — constructor parameters, method parameters, setters, and even things returned from methods of objects passed to the CUT (such as the car class calling _engine.GetTemperature() in the example in this paragraph).

In contrast, there is also "active collaboration," where the CUT takes responsibility for getting its own input. This is input that you cannot control when instantiating the class. An example of this is a call to some singleton or public static method in the CUT. The only way that you can reassume control is by not calling the method in which it occurs. If static/singleton calls occur in the constructor, you simply cannot test or even instantiate this class without it doing whatever the static code entails. If it retrieves values from static state, you have no control over those values (short of mocking up the application's global state).

A second form of active collaboration is the "new" operator. This is very similar to static state in that when you create the CUT, you have no control over this kind of input to the CUT. Imagine if Car new-ed up its own Engine and queried it for temperature. There would be absolutely no way that you could have any effect on this operation in the car class short of not instantiating it. Like static calls, object instantiation renders your CUTs a non-negotiable, "take it or leave it" proposition. You can have them with all of their instantiated objects and global state or you can write your own, buddy.

Not all inputs to a class are created equal. There are a CUT's passive inputs, in which the CUT cedes control to you. And then there are the CUT's active inputs that it controls and on which it does not allow you to interpose in any way. As it turns out, it is substantially easier to test CUTs with exclusively passive collaboration/input and difficult or even impossible to test CUTs with active collaboration. This is simply because you cannot isolate actively collaborating CUTs.

Literals: Too Simple to Need Test Doubles

There's still a little bit of work to do before we discuss test doubles in earnest. First, we have to talk about inputs that are too simple to require stand-ins: literals. The PrimeFinder test above is the perfect example of this. It's performing a mathematical operation using an integer input, so what we're interested in testing is known input-output pairs in a functional sense. As such, we just need to know what to pass in, to pass that value in, and then to assert that we get the expected return value.

In a strict sense, we could refer to this as a form of test double. After all, we're doing a non-production exercise with the API, so the value we're passing in is fake, in a sense. But that's a little formal for my taste. It's easier just to think in terms of literals almost always being too simple to require any sort of substitution of behavior.

An interesting exception to this the null literal (of null type) or the default value of a non-nullable type. In many cases, you may actually want to be testing this as an input since null and 0 tend to be particularly interesting inputs and the source of corner cases. However, in some cases, you may be supplying what is considered the simplest form of test double: the dummy value. A dummy value is something you pass into a function to say, "I don't care what this is and I'm just passing in something to make the compiler happy." An example of where you might do this is passing null to a constructor of an object instance when you just want to make assertions as to what some of its property values initialize to.

Simple/Value Objects and Passing in Friendlies

Next up for consideration is the concept of a "test stub," or what I'll refer to in the general sense as a "friendly."

Take a look at this code:

```
1    public class Car
2    {
3        public int EngineTemperature { get; private set; }
4
5        public Car(Engine engine)
6        {
7            EngineTemperature = engine.
     TemperatureInFahrenheit;
8        }
9    }
10   public class Engine
11   {
12       public int TemperatureInFahrenheit { get; set; }
13   }
```

Here is an incredibly simple implementation of the car-engine pair I described earlier. Car is passed an Engine and it queries that Engine for a local value that it exposes. Let's say that I now want to test that behavior. I want to test that Car's EngineTemperature property is equal to Engine's temperature in Fahrenheit. What do you think is a good test to write? Something like this, maybe –

| 1<br>2<br>3<br>4<br>5<br>6<br>7<br>8<br>9 | ```
[TestMethod]
public void EngineTemperature_Initializes_
Value_Returned_By_Engine()
{
    const int engineTemperatureFromEngine = 200;

    Engine engine = new Engine()
{       TemperatureInFahrenheit =
engineTemperatureFromEngine };
    var car = new Car(engine);

    Assert.AreEqual<int>(engineTemperatureFro
mEngine, car.EngineTemperature);
}
``` |

Here, we're setting up the engine instance in such a way as that we control what it provides to Car when Car uses it. We know by inspecting the code for Car that Car is going to ask Engine for its TemperatureInFahrenheit value, so we set that value to a known commodity, allowing us to compare in the Assert. To put it another way, we're supplying input indirectly to Car by setting up Engine and telling Engine what to give to Car. It's important to note that this is only possible because Car accepts Engine as an argument. If Car instantiated Engine in its constructor, *it would not be possible to isolate Car* because any test of Car's initial value would necessarily also be a test of Engine, making the test an integration test rather than a unit test.

Creating Bona Fide Mocks

That's all well and good, but what if the engine class were more complicated or just written differently? What if the way to get the temperature was to call a method and that method went and talked to a file or a database or something? Think of how badly the testing for this is going to go:
```

```
    public class Car
1   {
2      public int EngineTemperature { get; private set; }
3
4      public Car(Engine engine)
5      {
6              EngineTemperature = engine.
7   TemperatureInFahrenheit;
8      }
9   }
10     public class Engine
11     {
12        public int TemperatureInFahrenheit
13        {
14           get
15           {
16                var stream = new StreamReader(@"C:\
17   whatever.txt");
18                return int.Parse(stream.ReadLine());
19           }
20        }
    }
```

Now when we instantiate a car and query its engine temperature property, suddenly file contents are being read into memory, and, as I've already covered, File I/O is a definite no-no in a unit test. So I suppose we're hosed. As soon as Car tries to read Engine's temperature, we're going to explode — or we're going to succeed, which is even worse because now you'll have a unit test suite that depends on the machine it's running on having the file C:\whatever. txt on it and containing an integer as its first line.

But what if we got creative the way we did at the end of the last chapter? Let's make the TemperatureInFahrenheit property virtual and then declare the following class:

```
1      public class FakeEngine : Engine
2      {
3          private int _temperature;
4
5          public override int TemperatureInFahrenheit
6          {
7              get { return _temperature; }
8          }
9
10         public FakeEngine(int temperature)
11         {
12             _temperature = temperature;
13         }
```

This class is test friendly because it doesn't contain any file I/O at all and it inherits from Engine, overriding the offending methods. Now we can write the following unit test:

```
1      [TestMethod]
2      public void EngineTemperature_Initializes_Value_
       Returned_By_Engine()
3      {
4          const int engineTemperatureFromEngine = 200;
5          Engine engine = new FakeEngine(engineTempe
       ratureFromEngine);
6          var car = new Car(engine);
7
8          Assert.AreEqual<int>(engineTemperatureFrom
9      Engine, car.EngineTemperature);
       }
```

If this seems a little weird to you, remember that our goal here is to test the car class and not the engine class. All that the car class knows about Engine is that it wants its TemperatureInFahrenheit property. It doesn't (and shouldn't) care how or where this comes from internally to Engine — file I/O, constructor parameter, secret ink, whatever. And when testing the car class, you certainly don't care. Another way to think of this is that you're saying, "assuming that Engine tells Car that the engine temperature is 200, we want to assert that Car's EngineTemperature property is 200." In this fashion, we have isolated the car class and are testing only its functionality.

This kind of test double and testing technique is known as a fake. We're creating a fake engine to stand-in for the real one. It's not simple enough to be a dummy or a stub, since it's a real, bona fide different class instead of a doctored version of an existing one. I realize that the terminology for the different kinds of test doubles can be a little confusing, so here's a helpful taxonomy of them.

Mocking Frameworks

The last step in the world of test doubles is to get to actual mock objects. If you stop and ponder the fake approach from the last section a bit, a problem might occur to you. The problem has to do with long-term maintenance of code. I remember, many moons ago when I discovered the power of polymorphism for creating fake objects, that I thought it was the greatest thing under the sun. Obviously there was at least one fake per test class with dependency, and sometimes there were multiple dependencies. And I didn't always stop there — I might define three or four different variants of the fake, each having a method that behaved differently for the test in question. In one fake, TemperatureInFarenheit would return a passed in value, but in another, it would throw an exception. Oh, there were so many fakes — I was swimming in fakes for classes and fakes for interfaces.

And they were awesome...until I added a method to the interface they implemented or changed behavior in the class they inherited. And then, oh, the pain. I would have to go and change dozens of classes. And then there was also the fact that all of this faking took up a whole lot of space. My test classes were littered with nested classes of fakes. It was fun at first, but the maintenance became a drudgery. But don't worry, because my gift to you is to spare you that pain.

What if I told you that you could implement interfaces and inherit from classes anonymously without actually creating source code that did this? I'm oversimplifying a bit, but as you start to grasp the concept of mocking frameworks, this kind of "dynamic interface implementation/inheritance" is the easiest way to reason about what it's doing from a practical perspective without getting bogged down in more complicated concepts like reflection and direct work with byte-code and other bits of black magic.

As an example of this in action, take a look at how I go about testing Car and Engine with the difficult dependency. The first thing that I do is delete the fake class because there's no need for it. The next thing I do is write a unit test, using a framework called JustMock by Telerik. (This is currently my preferred mocking framework for C#.)

```
[TestMethod]
public void EngineTemperature_Initializes_Value_Returned_By_Engine()
{
    const int engineTemperatureFromEngine = 200;

    var engine = Mock.Create<Engine>();
    engine.Arrange(e => e.TemperatureInFahrenheit).Returns(engineTemperatureFromEngine);

    var car = new Car(engine);

    Assert.AreEqual<int>(engineTemperatureFromEngine, car.EngineTemperature);
}
```

Notice that instead of instantiating an engine, I now invoke a static method on a class called Mock that takes care of creating my dynamic inheritor for me. Mock.Create() is what creates the equivalent of FakeEngine. On the next line, I invoke an (extension) method called Arrange that creates an implementation of the property for me as well. What I'm saying, in plain English, is "take this mock engine and arrange it such that the TemperatureInFahrenheit property returns 200." I've done all of this in one line of code instead of adding an entire nested class. And, best of all, I don't need to change this mock if I decide to change some behavior in the base class or add a new method.

Truly, once you get used to the concept of mocking, you'll never go back. It will become your best friend for the purposes of mocking out dependencies of any real complexity. But temper your enthusiasm just a bit. It isn't a good idea to use mocking frameworks for simple dependencies like the PrimeFinder example. The lite version of JustMock that I've used and many others won't even allow it, and even if they did, that's way too much ceremony — just pass in real objects and literals, if you can reasonably.

The idea of injecting dependencies into classes (what I've called "passive" and "semi-passive" collaboration) is critical to mocking and unit testing. All basic mocking frameworks operate on the premise that you're using this style of collaboration and that your classes are candidates for polymorphism (either interfaces or overridable classes). You can't mock things like primitives and you can't mock sealed/final classes.

There are products out there called isolation frameworks that will grant you the ability to mock pretty much everything — primitives, sealed/final classes, statics/singletons and even the new operator. These are powerful (and often long-running, resource-intensive) tools that have their place, but that place is, in my opinion, at the edges of your code base. You can use this to mock File.Open() or new SqlConnection() or some GUI component to get the code at the edge of your application under test.

But using it to test your own application logic is a path that's fraught with danger. It's sort of like fixing a broken leg with morphine. Passively collaborating CUTs have seams in them that allow easy configuration of behavior changes and a clear delineation of responsibilities. Actively collaborating CUTs lack these things and are thus much more brittle and difficult to separate and modify. The fact that you can come up with a scheme allowing you to test the latter doesn't eliminate these problems — it just potentially masks them. I will say that isolating your coupled, actively collaborating code and testing it is better than not testing it, but neither one is nearly as good as factoring toward passive collaboration.

CHAPTER 7

OVERCOMING INERTIA AND OBJECTIONS

N ow that you're familiar with the topic and reasonably well versed in it (particularly if you've been practicing over the course of reading this book), I'd like to use that familiarity to discuss why unit testing makes sense in terms that you now better understand. And beyond that, I'd like to discuss how you can use this sense to overcome inertia and objections that others may have.

The Case for Unit Tests

Alright, so this is the part where I offer you a laundry list, right? This is where I say that unit tests improve code quality, document your code, exercise your API, promote (or at least correlate with) good design, help you break problems into manageable chunks, expose problems earlier when finding them is cheaper – the list goes on. And I believe that all of these things are true. But after a number of years of faithfully writing unit tests and practicing test-driven development (TDD), I think that I can offer those as appetizers or footnotes in the face of the real benefit: they allow you to refactor your code without fear or hesitation.

First to Contend With: Inertia

Inertia could probably be categorized as an objection, but I'm going to treat it separately since it manifests in a different way. Objections to doing something are essentially counterarguments to it. They may be lame counterarguments or excellent counterarguments, but either way, they take an active position. Inertia doesn't. It's either ambivalence or passive-aggressive resistance. To illustrate the difference, consider the following exchanges:

Alice: We should start trying to get our code under test. Bob: Unit testing is stupid and a complete waste of time.

versus

Alice: We should start trying to get our code under test. Bob: Yeah, that'd be nice. We should do that at some point.

The former is a strident (and obtuse) counterargument while the latter is an example of inactivity by inertia. In the second exchange, Bob either thinks unit testing is a good idea — but just not now — or he's blowing sunshine at Alice so that she'll leave him alone and stop stumping for change (i.e., he's taking the passive-aggressive approach).

In either case, the best way to overcome inertia is to counteract it with activity of your own. Inertia is the byproduct of the developer (and human, in general) tendency to get stuck in a rut of doing the comfortable and familiar. Overcoming it within your group is usually just a matter of creating a new rut for them. This isn't necessarily an easy thing to do. You'll have to write the tests, make sure they stay up to date, demonstrate the benefits to anyone who will listen and probably spend some time teaching others how to do it. But if you persevere and your only obstacle is inertia, sooner or later test writing will become the new normal. You'll get there.

Red Herrings and Stupid Objections

About a year ago, <u>I blogged about a guy who made a silly claim that he wrote a lot of unit tests but didn't check them in</u>. The reasoning behind this, as detailed in the chapter, was completely fatuous. But that's to be expected since the purpose of this claim wasn't to explain a calculated approach but rather to cover a lack of knowledge — the knowledge of how to write unit tests.

This sort of chapteruring is the province of threatened <u>expert beginners</u>. It's the kind of thing that happens when the guy in charge understands that unit testing is widely considered to be table stakes for software development professionalism but has no idea how it works. As such, he believes that he has to come up with a rationale for why he's never bothered to learn how to do it, but he's handicapped in inventing an explanation that makes sense by virtue of the fact that he has no idea what he's talking about. This results in statements like the following:

- Unit tests prevent you from adapting to new requirements.

- Testing takes too much time.

- It wouldn't work with our style of writing code.

- You're not going to catch every bug, so why bother?

- Writing all of your tests before writing any code is dumb.

- Management/customers wouldn't like it and wouldn't want to pay for it.

I obviously can't cover all such possible statements, but use the smell test. If it sounds incredible or stupid, it probably is, and you're likely dealing with someone who is interested in preserving his alpha status more than creating good work product. To be frank, if you're in an environment like that, you're probably best off practicing your craft on the sly. You can write tests and keep quiet about it or even keep them in your own personal source control (I have done both at times in my career when in this situation) to prevent people from impeding your own career development. But the best longer term strategy is to keep your eyes and ears open for other projects to work on that will provide you with more latitude to set policies. Do an open source project in your spare time, grab an opportunity to develop a one-off tool for your group or maybe even consider looking for a job at an organization a little more up to speed with current software development practices. You can stay and fight the good fight, but I don't recommend it in the long run. It'll wear you down, and you're unlikely to win many arguments with people that don't let a lack of knowledge stop them from claiming expertise on a subject.

"I Don't Know How to Unit Test"

With inertia and silliness set aside, let's move on to legitimate objections to the practice. At first blush, you may be inclined to scoff at the objection, "I don't understand it," particularly in an industry often dominated by people unwilling to concede that their knowledge is lacking in the slightest bit in any way whatsoever. But don't scoff — this is a perfectly reasonable objection. It's hard and often unwise simply to start doing something with professional stakes when you don't know what you're doing.

If the people around you admit to not knowing how to do it, this earnest assessment often indicates at least some willingness to learn. This is great news and something you can work with. Start teaching yourself how to do it so that you can help others. Watch Pluralsight videos and show them to your coworkers as well. If your group is amenable to it, you can even set aside some time to practice as a group or to bring in consultants to get you off to a good start. This is an objection that can easily be turned into an asset.

"It Doesn't Work With the Way I Code"

I originally wrote this chapter because of a comment in the very first chapter, and this section is the one that addresses that comment. Arguments of this form are ones I've heard quite frequently over the years, and the particulars of the coding style in question vary, but the common thread is the idea that unit testing creates friction with an established routine. This isn't the same as "I don't know how to unit test" because the people who say this generally do know how to write tests — they must or else they wouldn't know anything about the subject and would make up expert-beginner-style stupid excuses. It also isn't the same as the inertia objection because they're saying, "I was willing to try, but I find that this impedes me," rather than, "meh, I dunno, I like my routine."

My short answer to someone who has this objection is, to put it bluntly, "change the way you code." Whatever the specifics of your approach, when you're done, you don't wind up with a fast-executing safety net of tests that you trust — tests that document your intentions, keep your code flexible, help prevent regressions, and force your design to be easy to use and decoupled. People who code differently than you do, in that they unit test, wind up with those things. So figure out a way to be one of those people.

On a deeper level, though, I understand this objection because it hits closer to home. I was never the type to bluster like an expert beginner, nor am I prone in the slightest to inertia. (I am pretty much the opposite, frequently biting off more than I can chew.) The other objections never really applied to me, but this one did both prior to starting to write tests and prior to adopting TDD as my exclusive approach to developing. You can read that latter perspective from my very early days of blogging. Years ago, I chafed at the prospect of unit testing because spending the extra time took me out of the 'flow' of my coding, and I balked at TDD because I thought "why would I start writing unit tests for this code when it might be refactored completely later?" In other words, neither one of these worked with my approach.

But in both cases, I relented eventually and changed the way I coded. I didn't just one day say, "well, I guess I'll just start writing code differently from now on." What happened instead was that I realized that a lot of really bright people and prominent names in the industry had coding and design styles that were compatible with writing tests, so it was at least worth trying things their way. It wasn't a matter of doing something because the cool kids were doing it or resolving to change my ways. Rather, I thought to myself, "I'll see what all the fuss is about. Then, I'll either like it, or I'll go back to my way of doing things armed with much better arguments as to why my way is better." So I poured myself into a different way of doing things, forced myself to keep at it even though it was slow and awkward, and, wouldn't you know it, I eventually came to prefer it.

Convincing people in your group to follow that lead is not going to be easy, but it is doable. The best way to do it is to earn their respect and show them results. If your code is cleaner and freer of bugs and your past projects are easy to adapt and modify, people are going to notice and ask you what your secret is, and you'll be in a position to show them. It may seem improbable to you now, but you can go from being a person quietly teaching yourself to unit test on the side to one of the key leaders in a software department relatively quickly. You just have to commit yourself to continuous improvement and moving toward proven, effective techniques. Unit testing is just one such technique, but it is a powerful and important one.

CHAPTER 8

TEST SUITE MANAGEMENT AND BUILD INTEGRATION

S o far, I've talked quite a lot about how and when (and when not) to write unit tests. I've offered up some techniques for helping you isolate the classes that you want to test, including the use of test doubles. And finally, I offered some advice on how to get people to leave you alone and let you write tests. So now I'd like to turn around and offer some advice beyond just writing the things. You need to live with them, manage them and leverage them over the course of time.

Managing the Suite

You've built them. So, now what? At some point, you'll wonder exactly when you're getting started. For the first few or even few dozen classes you test, you'll alternate between some exasperation at spending extra time doing something new and satisfaction at, well, doing something new. But then, at some point, you'll be sitting around and notice that your test suite has like 400 tests and think, "wow, that's a lot of code… do I really want all this?"

That feeling will hit you even harder when you go to change something under a tight deadline and your real quick change makes a test go red. You're pretty sure the test is broken because it was testing the old way of doing things, so you really just want to comment out the test and wonder why it's such a pain to change the code. Why do you have to waste so much time to change one line of code?

The answer to these questions lies in both practice and effective test suite management. If you let the unit test suite become a boat anchor, it will drag you down. Your frustration will be real and reasonable, rather than just a temporary product of you being in a hurry and unfamiliar with working in a code base under test. You need to take care to prevent this from happening, and I'm going to tell you how in this section.

Name Your Tests Clearly and Be Wordy

When you're writing a unit test, you're looking at code. But when you're running your test suite, you aren't most of the time. When you're trying to understand why a run or a build failed, you're never looking at code. When the test suite is failing, you don't want to waste time figuring out why. And having to open the IDE, navigate to the test, read the code and figure out the problem is a waste of time.

Don't give your test methods names like "Test24" or "CustomerTest" or something. Instead, give them names like "Customer_IsValid_Returns_False_When_Customer_SocialSecurityNumber_Is_

Empty". That method name may seem ridiculous, especially if you're used to giving methods short names, but trust me, you'll be thankful for it. When your build is failing, which of these method names would you rather see an X next to? Would you rather be saying "looks like test 24 is failing," or would you rather be saying, "oh, I wonder why someone made it so that an empty SSN is now considered valid?" If you say the first one, you're lying.

This may seem unimportant in the scheme of things, but it's the difference between associating frustration and confusion with your test suite and viewing it as a warning system for potentially undesirable changes. The test suite needs to be communicating clearly to you what's wrong. Descriptive test names help do that, and they help you identify whether it's your code or the test itself that needs to be changed in the face of changing requirements.

Make Your Test Suite Fast

Ruthlessly delete and cull out slow tests. I can't say it more plainly than that. A good test suite runs in seconds, max. If yours starts to take minutes, or God forbid, hours, then it's rotting and becoming useless to you. Think of it this way — if it takes several minutes to run the test suite, how often are you going to do it? Every time you make a change, or just when you check in? If it takes hours, will you ever run it voluntarily?

If your test suite takes a long time to run, nobody will run it. Short feedback loops are of paramount importance to developers, and we optimize for efficiency. If the unit test suite is inefficient, we'll find other ways to get feedback. As such, it is incredibly important to ensure that your test suite always runs quickly. Treat it as if the rest of your team were waiting for any legitimate excuse not to use the test suite, and don't let inefficiency be that excuse.

Test Code is First Class Code

A common mistake that I see among those relatively new to testing is test code that's something of a mess. The code will be brittle, heavily duplicated, weird, and hard to read. In short, your tests and test classes will contain code that you wouldn't be caught dead putting into production.

Don't do that. Treat your test code as if it were any other code. Eliminate duplication. Factor common functionality out into methods. Be descriptive with naming and with the flow of the method. Keep that code clean. I get that there's a desire when it comes to testing to make as much of a mess as possible in the "bug bash" sense of throwing chaos at the situation and proving that your code can handle it, but the chaos needs to be controlled. You can control it by keeping your test code clean and maintainable. If the tests are clean and easy to maintain, people won't mind going in periodically to make an adjustment. If they're unruly, people will get annoyed and comment them out or stop running them.

Have a Single Assertion per Test

This is a subtle one, but it also goes toward maintainability. If you start writing tests that have 20 asserts in them, you may feel good that you're exercising a whole section of the code, but really you're making things hard for yourself later. If all 20 tests pass (or at least the first 19), then all will be executed. But if the first one fails, none of the rest get executed. This means that in test methods with lots of asserts, it's not always clear where they're failing, which means it's not always clear what's going wrong.

In order for your test suite to be an asset, it has to be a clear indicator of what's going wrong. Which would you find more useful in your car: a series of many different lights with helpful diagrams that lit up to indicate a problem, or one unlabeled red light that came on whenever anything at all was wrong? If you had that latter light and it could mean anything from your gas being low to you being out of wiper fluid to imminent destruction of your transmission, I bet you'd just start ignoring it after a while.

Don't Share State Between Your Tests

There is no more surefire way to drive yourself insane at some future date than by storing some kind of application state among unit tests being executed. What I mean is if you have some test A that sets a global counter variable to 1, and then you have another test B that depends on the global counter being set to 1 in order for it to succeed, you are in for a world of hurt.

The problem is that there is no guarantee that the unit test runner will execute the tests in any particular order. What's likely to happen is that your tests get executed in a particular order whenever you run them on your machine, so everything goes fine. But when the build machine runs them they fail. Weird. So you check them on your friend Bob's machine, and they pass there. But on Alice's machine, they fail. If you didn't already know why this was happening because I just told you, can you imagine how much of your hair you'd pull out? You'd probably be checking the IDE version on those machines, compiler information, OS settings, and who knows what else. It'd be a wild goose chase.

And imagine if it worked on everyone's machine initially and then six months later started failing occasionally on the build machine. Machine isn't the only failing dimension — there's also time. So please, whatever you do, do not have your unit tests depend on the execution of a previous test. This practice, more than any other, is likely to lead to a rage-quitting of unit testing as a practice where you simply take all of them out of the build.

Encourage Others and Keep Them Invested

This sounds like a strange one to round out the section, but it's important. If you're the only one fighting the good fight with unit tests, it becomes daunting and exasperating. Everyone else's reaction to failing tests is annoyance and they're waiting for excuses just to stop altogether. You wind up feeling that you're in an adversarial relationship with the team (I speak from experience here). But if you get others to buy in, you're not shouldering the burden alone and you have help keeping the suite healthy and helpful.

Build Integration

When you first start out unit testing, the tests will be sort of disorganized and haphazard. You'll write a few to get the hang of it and then maybe discard them. After a bit of that, you'll start checking them into your solution (unless you're an <u>incorrigible weirdo or a liar</u>). You do that, the suite grows and, ideally, everyone is running it locally to keep things clean and be notified of potential breaking changes.

But you have to take it beyond that at some point if you want to realize the full value of the unit tests. They can't just be a thing everyone remembers to do locally on pain of nagging emails or because someone will buy the team donuts or some other peer-pressure-oriented demerit system. Failing unit tests have to have real (read: automated) consequences. And the best way to do this is to make it so that failing unit tests mean a failing build.

If you're in a shop that's not as formal, this may be difficult at first. One handicap may be that you're reading this and saying "what do you mean by 'the build?'" If what you do is write code and take some kind of executable out of your project's output directory on your machine and push it to a server or to your users, you've got some work to do before you think about integrating unit tests. You need a build. A build is an automated process by which your source code is turned into a production-ready, deployable package. And it's automated in the sense that it doesn't involve you hitting Ctrl-Shift-B or Ctrl-F6 or whatever you do manually in your IDE to build. The Build, with a capital B, is a process that checks your code out of source control, builds it, runs checks and whatever else is necessary, perhaps increments the versioning of the executables, etc., and then spits out the final product that will be pushed to a server or burned onto a DVD or whatever. If you want to read more about build tools, you can google around about TeamCity, CruiseControl, TFS, FinalBuilder, Jenkins etc. And you don't have to use a product like that — you can create your own using shell scripts or code if you choose.

Because of all the different options when it comes to programming languages, unit test technologies and build tools, I'm not going to offer a tutorial on how to integrate unit tests into your build. To be comprehensive, I'd need to give dozens of such tutorials. But what I will say is that your integration is going to take the same basic format no matter what tools you're using. The build is a series of steps that passes if everything goes smoothly and the deliverables are ultimately generated. If a step in the build fails, then the build itself fails. What you need to do is add a step that involves running the unit tests. With this in place, you're creating a situation where any failing unit test means that the entire build fails.

Conceptually, this is pretty straightforward. Unit test runners can be run in command line fashion and they'll generate a return value of some kind. So the build tool needs to examine the test runner's output for an error code. If it finds one, it puts the brakes on the whole operation.

It may seem extreme at first to torpedo the whole build because of a failing unit test, but when you think about it, what else should possibly happen? Why would you want a process that allowed you to ship code knowing that it was defective in a way that it didn't used to be? That's amateur hour. And, what's more is that if your team starts understanding that failed unit tests mean a failed build they'll be sure to run the tests before check-in so that they don't fail. It will become a natural part of your process, and the quality of your software will be dramatically improved for it.

CHAPTER 9

TIPS AND TRICKS FOR NEW AND VETERAN UNIT TESTERS

Structure the Test Names for Readability Beyond Just Descriptive Names

The first step in making your unit tests true representations of business statements is to give them nice, descriptive names. Some people do this with "given, when, then" verbiage, and others are simply verbose. I like mine to read like conversational statements, and this creates almost comically long names like "GetCustomerAddress_ Returns_Null_When_Customer_Is_Partially_Registered."   I've been given flack for things like this during my career and you might get some as well, but you know what? No one is ever going to ask you what this test is checking. And if it fails, no one is ever going to say, "I wonder why the unit test suite is failing." They're going to know that it's failing because GetCustomerAddress is returning something other than null for a partially registered customer.

When you're writing unit tests, it's easy to gloss over names of the tests the way you might with methods in your production code. And, while I would never advocate glossing over naming anywhere, you *especially* don't want to do it with unit tests because unit test names are going to wind up in a report generated by your build machine or your IDE, whereas production methods won't unless you're using a static analysis tool with reporting, like NDepend.

But it goes beyond simply giving tests descriptive names. Come up with a good scheme for having your tests be as readable as possible in these reports. This is a scheme from Phil Haack that makes a lot of sense.

I adopted a variant of it after reading the chapter, and have been using it to eliminate duplication in the names of my unit tests. This consideration of where, how, and by whom the test names will be read is important. I'm not being more specific here simply because how you do this exactly will depend on your language, IDE, testing framework, build technology, etc. But the message is the same regardless: make sure that you name your tests in such a way to maximize the value for those who are reading reports of the test names and results.

Create an Instance Field or Property Called "Target"

This one took a while to grow on me, but it eventually did and it did big time. Take a look at the code below, originally from a series I did on TDD:

```
1    [TestClass]
2    public class BowlingTest
3    {
4      [TestClass]
5      public class Constructor
6      {
7
8        [TestMethod, Owner("ebd"), TestCategory("Proven"), TestCategory("Unit")]
9        public void Initializes_Score_To_Zero()
10       {
11         var scoreCalculator = new BowlingScoreCalculator();
12
13         Assert.AreEqual<int>(0, scoreCalculator.Score);
14       }
15     }
16
17     [TestClass]
18     public class BowlFrame
19     {
20       private static BowlingScoreCalculator Target { get; set; }
21
22       [TestInitialize()]
23       public void BeforeEachTest()
24       {
25         Target = new BowlingScoreCalculator();
26       }
27
28       [TestMethod, Owner("ebd"), TestCategory("Proven"), TestCategory("Unit")]
29       public void With_Throws_0_And_1_Results_In_Score_1()
30       {
31         var frame = new Frame(0, 1);
32         Target.BowlFrame(frame);
33
34         Assert.AreEqual<int>(frame.FirstThrow + frame.SecondThrow, Target.Score);
35       }
36
37       [TestMethod, Owner("ebd"), TestCategory("Proven"), TestCategory("Unit")]
38       public void With_Throws_2_And_3_Results_In_Score_5()
39       {
40         var frame = new Frame(2, 3);
41         Target.BowlFrame(frame);
42
43         Assert.AreEqual<int>(frame.FirstThrow + frame.SecondThrow, Target.Score);
44       }
45
46       [TestMethod, Owner("ebd"), TestCategory("Proven"), TestCategory("Unit")]
47       public void Sets_Score_To_2_After_2_Frames_With_Score_Of_1_Each()
48       {
49         var frame = new Frame(1, 0);
50         Target.BowlFrame(frame);
51         Target.BowlFrame(frame);
52
53         Assert.AreEqual<int>(frame.Total + frame.Total, Target.Score);
54       }
55
56       [TestMethod, Owner("ebd"), TestCategory("Proven"), TestCategory("Unit")]
57       public void Sets_Score_To_Twenty_After_Spare_Then_Five_Then_Zero()
58       {
59         var firstFrame = new Frame(9, 1);
60         var secondFrame = new Frame(5, 0);
```

```
61
62            Target.BowlFrame(firstFrame);
63            Target.BowlFrame(secondFrame);
64
65            Assert.AreEqual<int>(20, Target.Score);
66        }
67
68        [TestMethod, Owner("ebd"), TestCategory("Proven"), TestCategory("Unit")]
69        public void Sets_Score_To_25_After_Strike_Then_Five_Five()
70        {
71            var firstFrame = new Frame(10, 0);
72            var secondFrame = new Frame(6, 4);
73
74            Target.BowlFrame(firstFrame);
75            Target.BowlFrame(secondFrame);
76
77            Assert.AreEqual<int>(30, Target.Score);
78        }
79      }
80    }
81
82    public class BowlingScoreCalculator
83    {
84      private readonly Frame[] _frames = new Frame[10];
85
86      private int _currentFrame;
87
88      private Frame LastFrame { get { return _frames[_currentFrame - 1]; } }
89
90      public int Score { get; private set; }
91
92      public void BowlFrame(Frame frame)
93      {
94        AddMarkBonuses(frame);
95
96        Score += frame.Total;
97        _frames[_currentFrame++] = frame;
98      }
99
100     private void AddMarkBonuses(Frame frame)
101     {
102       if (WasLastFrameAStrike()) Score += frame.Total;
103       else if (WasLastFrameASpare()) Score += frame.FirstThrow;
104     }
105
106     private bool WasLastFrameAStrike()
107     {
108       return _currentFrame > 0 && LastFrame.IsStrike;
```

If you look at the nested test class corresponding to the BowlFrame method, you'll notice that I have a class level property called "Target" and I have a method called "BeforeEachTest" that runs at the start of each test and instantiates Target. I used to be more of a purist in wanting all unit test methods to be completely and utterly self-contained, but after a while, I couldn't deny the readability of this approach.

Using Target cuts out at least one line of pointless (and repetitive) instantiation inside each test. It also unifies the naming of the thing you're testing. In other words, throughout the entire test class, interaction with the class under test is extremely obvious. Another ancillary benefit to this approach is that if you need to change the instantiation logic by, say, adding a constructor parameter; you do it one place only and you don't have to go limping all over your test class, doing it everywhere.

I highly recommend that you consider adopting this convention for your tests.

Use the Test Initialize (and Tear-Down) for Intuitive Naming and Semantics

Along these same lines, I recommend giving some consideration to test initialization and tear-down, if necessary. I name these methods "BeforeEachTest" and "AfterEachTest" for the sake of clarity. In the previous section, I talked about this for instantiating Target, but this is also a good place to instantiate other common dependencies such as mock objects or to build friendly instances that you pass to constructors and methods.

This approach also creates a unified and symmetric feel in your test classes, and that kind of predictability tends to be invaluable. People often debug production code, but they are far more likely to initially contemplate unit tests by inspecting them, so predictability here is as important as it is anywhere.

Keep Your Mind on AAA

AAA. Arrange, Act, Assert. (Or, as I once referred to it as, <u>setup, poke, verify.</u>) Think of your unit tests in these terms at all times and you'll do well. The basic anatomy of a unit test is that you set up the world that you're testing to exist in some situation that matters to you, then you do something, then you verify that what you did produced the result you expect. A real-world equivalent might be that you put a metal rod in the freezer for two hours (arrange), take it out and stick your tongue on it (act), and verify that you can't remove your tongue from it (assert).

If you don't think of your tests this way, they tend to meander a lot. You'll do things like run through lists of arguments checking for exceptions or calling a rambling series of methods to make sure "nothing bad happens." This is the unit test equivalent of babbling, and you don't want to do that. Each test should have some specific, detailed arrangement, some easily describable action and some clear assertion.

Keep your Instantiation Logic in One Place

In a previous section, I suggested using the test runner's initialize method to do this, but the important thing is that you do it somehow. I have lived the pain of having to do find/replace or other, more manual corrections when modifying constructors for classes that I was instantiating in every unit test for dozens or even hundreds of tests.

Your unit test code is no different than production code in that duplication is your enemy. If you're instantiating your class under test again and again and again, you're going to suffer when you need to change the instantiation logic — or else you're going to avoid changing it to avoid suffering. And altering your design to make copy-and-paste programming less painful is like treating an infected cut by drinking alcohol until you black out and forget about your infected cut.

Don't Be Exhaustive (You Don't Need to Test All Inputs — Just Interesting Ones)

One thing I've seen occasionally with people new to unit testing, especially with those getting their heads around TDD, is a desire to start exhaustively unit testing for all inputs. For instance, let's say you're implementing a prime number finder as I described in my Pluralsight course on NCrunch and continuous testing. At what point have you written enough tests for prime finder? Is it when you've tested all inputs, 1 through 10? 1 through 100? All 32-bit integers?

I strongly advise against doing any of these things or even writing some test that iterates through a series of values in a loop testing for them. Instead, write as many tests as you need to tease out the algorithm if you're following TDD and, in the end, have as many tests as you need to cover interesting cases that you can think of. For me, off the top (TDD notwithstanding), I might pick a handful of primes to test and a handful of composite numbers — so maybe one small prime and composite and one large one of each that I looked up on the internet somewhere. There are other interesting values as well, such as negative numbers, one, and zero. I'd make sure it behaved correctly for each of these cases and then move on.

It might take some practice to fight the feeling that this is insufficient coverage, but you have to think less in terms of the set of all possible inputs and more in terms of the set of paths through your code. Test out corner cases, oddball conditions, potential "off-by-one" situations, and maybe one or two standard sorts of inputs. And remember, if later some kind of bug or deficiency is discovered, you can always add more test cases to your test suite. Your test suite is an asset, but it's also code that must be maintained. Don't overdo it. Test as much as necessary to make your intentions clear, guard against regressions, but don't do more than is needed.

Use a Continuous Testing Tool Like NCrunch

If you want to see just how powerful a continuous testing tool is, check out that Pluralsight video I did. Continuous testing is game changer. If you aren't familiar with continuous testing, you can read about it at the NCrunch website. The gist of it is that you get live, real-time feedback as to whether your unit tests are passing as you type.

Let that sink in for a minute: no running a unit test runner, no executing the tests in the IDE, and not even any building of the code. As you type, from one character to the next, the unit tests execute constantly and give you instantaneous feedback as to whether you're breaking things or not. So if you wander into your production code and delete a line, you should expect that you'll suddenly see red on your screen because you're breaking things (assuming you don't have useless lines of code).

I cannot overstate how much this will improve your efficiency. You will never go back once you get used to this.

Unit Tests Instead of the Console

Use unit tests instead of the console or whatever else you might use to do experimentation. Get comfortable with the format of the tests. Most developers have some quick way of doing experiments — scratchpads, if you will. If you make yours a unit test project, you'll get used to having unit tests as your primary feedback mechanism.

In the simplest sense, this is practice with the unit test paradigm, and that never hurts. In a more philosophical sense, you're starting to think of your code as a series of entry points that you can use for inspection and determining how things interact. And that's the real, longer term value — an understanding that good design involves seams in the code and unit tests let you access those seams.

Get Familiar With All of the Keyboard Shortcuts

Again, this is going to vary based on your environment, but make sure to learn whatever keyboard shortcuts and things your IDE offers to speed up test management and execution. The faster you are with the tests, the more frequently you'll execute them, the more you'll rely on them and the more you'll practice with them.

Your unit test suite should be a handy, well-worn tool and a comfortable safety blanket. It should feel right and be convenient and accessible. So anything you can do to wear it in, so to speak, will expedite this feeling. Take the time to learn these shortcuts and practice them — you won't regret it. Even if you have a continuous testing tool, you can benefit from learning the most efficient way to use it. Improvement is always possible.

General Advice

Cliché as it may sound and be, the best tip I can give you overall is to practice, practice, practice. Testing will be annoying and awkward at first, but it will become increasingly second nature as you practice. I know that it can be hard to get into or easy to leave by the wayside when you're staring at a deadline, but the practice will mitigate both considerations. You'll grow less frustrated and watch the barriers to entry get lower and, as you get good, you won't feel any inclination to stop unit testing when the stakes are high. In fact, with enough practice, that's when you'll feel it's most important. You will get there with enough effort — I promise.

CHAPTER 10

THE BUSINESS VALUE OF UNIT TESTS

Backstory

I worked for a consulting firm for a while. We didn't make anything particularly exciting — line-of-business applications and the like was about the extent of it. The billing model for clients was dead simple and resembled the way that lawyers charge; consultants had an hourly rate, and we kept diligent track of our time to the nearest quarter hour. There was a certain feel-good element to this oversimplification of knowledge work in the same way that it's pleasant to lean back, watch Superman defeat Lex Luthor and delight in a PG world where Good v Evil grudge matches always end with Good coming out the victor.

It's pleasant to think that writing software has the predictable, low-thought cadence of an activity like chopping wood where each 15 minutes spent produces a fairly constant amount of value to the recipient of the labor. (Cue background song, Lou Reed, "A Perfect Day") Chop for 15 minutes, collect $3, hand over X chopped logs. Chop for one hour, collect $12, hand over 4X chopped logs. Write software for 15 minutes; produce a working, 15 LOC application for $25. Write software for one hour; produce a working, 60 LOC application for $100. Oh, such a perfect day.

When I started at the company, I asked some people if they wrote unit tests. The answer was generally 'no,' and the justification for this was that you'd have to run it by the client and the client most likely wouldn't want to pay for you to write unit tests. What they meant by this was that, since we billed in quarter-hour increments and supplied invoices with detailed logs of all activity, it'd be sort of hard to sneak in 15 minutes of writing automated test code. Presumably, the fear was that the client would say, "What's this 'unit testing' stuff and why did you do it when you didn't say anything about it?" I say "presumably" because this wasn't the reason people didn't unit test at this company, just like whatever excuse they have at your company isn't the real reason for not unit testing there. The real reason is usually not knowing how to do it.

Why did I start out with this anecdote and its centerpiece of the quarter-hour billing and development cadence? Well, simply because software development is a creative exercise and far too spastic to flow along smoothly in a low-viscosity stream of lines of code per minute. You may sit and stare blankly at a computer screen while contemplating design for half an hour, code for four minutes, stare blankly again for an hour, code for 20 minutes, and then finish the product. So, 24 minutes — is that a billable half hour or 15 minutes? Closer to 30, I suppose. Do you count the blank staring? On the one hand, this was the real work — the knowledge work — in a way that the typing certainly wasn't. So should you bill one and a half hours instead and just count the typing as a brainless exercise? Or should you bill two hours because the work is a gestalt? I personally think that the answer is obvious and the gestalt billing model cuts right to the notion that software development is a holistic exercise that involves delivering a working product, and the breakdown may include typing; thinking; whiteboarding; searching Stack Overflow; debugging; squinting at a GUI; talking to another developer; going for a five minute walk for perspective; running a static analysis tool; tracking down a compiler warning; copying 422 files to a target directory; and, yes, my friend, unit testing.

Those are all things that you do as part of writing good software. And in a consulting paradigm, you wouldn't cut one of them out and say, "the client wouldn't want to pay for that." That's because the client *doesn't know what it's talking about* when you're under the software-writing hood — that's why they're paying you. They wouldn't want to pay for "searching Stack Overflow" or "squinting at the GUI" either, but you don't refuse to do those things when you're writing software. And so refusing to unit test for this same reason is a cop-out. When a younger developer at that firm asked me why I wrote unit tests and how I accounted for them in my billing, this was essentially the argument I gave — I asked him how he accounted for the time he spent compiling, debugging, and running the application and, bright guy that he is, he understood what I was saying immediately.

Core Business Value

This may seem like a roundabout and long introduction to this chapter, but it really cuts to the core of the business value proposition for unit tests. During development, why do developers compile, run and debug? Well, they do it to see if their code is doing what they think it should do. Write some code, then make sure it's doing what you expect. So why write unit tests? To make sure your code is doing what you expect, and to make sure it keeps doing what you expect via automation. The core business value of unit tests is that they serve as progress markers, sign chapters and guard rails on the road to an application that does what you expect.

Unit-tested applications are more predictable and better documented than their non-unit-tested counterparts (assuming the same amount of API documentation and commenting are done), and there is an enormous amount of business value in predictability and clarity of intent. With a good unit test suite, you'll know in minutes if you've introduced a regression bug. Without that unit test suite, when will you know? When you run the application GUI? When QA runs it a week later? When the customer runs it a month later? When something randomly goes haywire a year later? Each one of these delays becomes <u>exponentially more expensive</u>.

That's not the only value-add from a business perspective (and I'll list some other ones next), but it's the main one, as far as I'm concerned. It also explains why the notion that you need to carve out some extra time for unit tests and figure out whether the customer wants them or not is prechaptererous. Do you think the customer is going to get angry if you explain that part of your development process is to execute the code you just wrote to make sure it doesn't crash? If the answer to that is "no, of course not, that's ridiculous," then you also have the answer to whether or not a customer would care if you happened to automate that process.

Of course, one thing to bear in mind is that a customer may not want to pay for you to *learn on the job* to unit test, and that's a fair point. But if the customer (or your company, internally, if you aren't a consultant) doesn't want to foot the bill for this, then you should strongly consider picking it up on your own and then switching customers/companies if they don't buy in to something as fundamental as automating predictability. Unit tests are the software equivalent of accountants practicing double entry bookkeeping, doctors washing their hands, electricians turning power back on before leaving and plumbers doing the same with the water. Imagine if your plumber sweat welded a joint for your new shower; sized it up; said, "meh, I'm sure it's fine," and left without ever running the water. That's what tens of thousands of us do every day when we just assume some piece of code works because it worked a month ago and you don't remember touching it since then. Ship it? Meh, sure, whatever — it's probably fine. The business value of unit tests is a stronger assurance that we know what's going on than "meh, sure, whatever."

Ancillary Business Value

Here are some other ways in which unit tests add value to the business beyond confirming that the application behaves as expected.

First, unit tests tend to serve nicely as documentation. This may sound strange at first. You're probably thinking, "How is a bunch of code documentation when we have a whole activity associated with documenting our code?" Well, fact of the matter is that documentation in the form of writeups, code comments, instruction manuals, etc. tends to get out of date as the product ages. Unit tests, however, are never out of date because, if they were, the build would fail (or at least you'd see red when you ran them) and you'd be forced to go back and "fix the documentation." If you keep your unit test methods clean and give them good names as described in earlier chapters, they'll also read more like a book than like code, and they'll document purpose and intended behavior of the system.

Unit tests also guard against regression. When you write the tests, you're confirming that the software does what you expect it to at that moment. But what about later? Maybe later you forget what you intended in that moment or decide that you intended something different and you change the code. Will it still work? In a lot of legacy code bases, the answer to that question is "yikes — who knows?" With a thoughtfully unit-tested code base, you can rig it so that a test goes red if a design assumption that you made is no longer true. For instance, say you write some method with the intention that it never return null, and say that eventually you and your teammates build on this method and its assumed chapter-condition, grabbing values returned by the method and never checking for null before dereferencing them. If someone later modifies that method and adds a condition in which it returns null, the only thing standing between them and introducing a regression bug is a unit test that fails if that method returns null.

The practice of automated unit testing has after-the-fact benefits such as documentation and guards against regression bugs, but it also helps during the course of development by having a positive impact on your design. I've long been a fan of and have previously linked to this excellent talk by Michael Feathers called "The Deep Synergy Between Testability and Good Design." The general idea is that writing code with the knowledge that you're going to be writing tests for it (or practicing TDD) leads you to write small, factored classes and methods that are loosely coupled, and this practice in turn creates flexible and maintainable code. Or consider the converse, and think of how hard it is to write unit tests for giant, procedural methods and classes. Unit tests make it harder to do things that make your code awful.

Lastly, I'll throw in a benefit that summarizes my take on this entire subject and really drives things home. It's a huge bit of editorializing, but I feel somewhat entitled to it in my own conclusion. I believe that a serious piece of value added by unit testing is that it lends you or your group legitimacy and credibility. In this day and age, the question, "should you unit test your code?" is basically considered to be settled case law in the industry. So the question, to a large extent, boils down to whether you write tests or whether you have excuses, legitimate or otherwise. And there are legitimate ones, such as "I don't know how, yet." But in the end, don't be in the camp that has excuses.

Forget justifying what you or your organization has done up to this point, and imagine yourself as a customer of software development. You've got a budget, and you're looking to have some software written that you don't have time yourself to write. All other things being equal, which group do you hire? Do you hire a group that responds to "Do you unit test?" with "No, we don't think our customers would want that"? How about a group that responds with "Well, there's this database and this GUI and sometimes there's hardware, so we really can't"? Or do you hire a group that responds with, "We sure do, would you like to see some samples?" I bet it's the last one, if you're honest with yourself.

So be that last group. Add value to your users and your business. Write good software and consider your design carefully, and, just as importantly, automate the process of ensuring your software does what you think it does. Your credibility and the credibility of your software is at stake.

ABOUT THE AUTHOR

Erik Dietrich is the founder and principal of DaedTech LLC. He has a BS Degree in Computer Science from Carnegie Mellon University and a MS degree in the same from University of Illinois at Urbana-Champaign. Currently a systems architect with over ten years of experience in software architecture, design, implementation, and stabilizing/sustaining, Erik has a wide range of personal interests in addition to this area of expertise. These include home automation and home improvement, conceptual mathematics, literature, philosophy, and the sciences.

Printed in Great Britain
by Amazon